Emirates
The Middle East's Largest Airline

BABAK TAGHVAEE

Key Books

AIRLINES SERIES, VOLUME 22

Front cover image: Emirates is the world's largest operator of the Airbus A380. Two of the airline's A380-861s, including this example, A6-EUK, received a 'Journey To The Future' special livery. It is in Paris in November 2023. (Babak Taghvaee)

Title page image: Emirates has the greatest number of the world's largest passenger aircraft, the Airbus A380-800. This A380-861 with registration code (r/c) A6-EUB is one of them and is landing at Charles de Gaulle Airport, Paris, in September 2023. (Babak Taghvaee)

Contents page image: Emirates also has the greatest number of Boeing 777-300ER series of wide-body passenger aircraft. Prior to operating this series, the airline employed the Boeing 777-300 series. A6-EMN, a Boeing 777-31H was operated by Emirates between 1999 and 2017. It is next to the air traffic control tower at Dubai International Airport in February 2015. (Babak Taghvaee)

Back cover image: Emirates is also the world's largest operator of the Boeing 777-300ER series aircraft. This Boeing 777-31HER with r/c A6-ENG is one of them and is in Athens in September 2023. (Babak Taghvaee)

Published by Key Books
An imprint of Key Publishing Ltd
PO Box 100
Stamford
Lincs PE9 1XQ

www.keypublishing.com

ISBN 978 1 80282 874 0

Typeset by SJmagic DESIGN SERVICES, India.

Contents

Introduction

Established in 1985, Emirates is the largest airline in the Middle East and has a reputation for being one of the safest in the world. At the beginning of 2024, the Emirates Group had 260 passenger, cargo and business jets, of which 231 were airworthy. As the world's largest operator of Airbus A380-800s, these four-engined, wide-body passenger aircraft collectively logged an average 935 flights per week, transferring millions of passengers around the globe.

As of December 2023, Emirates operated 1,500 weekly departures on average from its passenger hub at Dubai International Airport and about 70 weekly freighter departures from Dubai World Central. Operating a fleet of modern and efficient wide-body aircraft, Emirates' global network spans 148 cities (including Dubai) in 79 countries/territories, facilitating trade and tourism links for the United Arab Emirates (UAE), and connecting the world through Dubai.

Emirates has a fleet of young and well-maintained passenger aircraft. As of December 2023, its passenger and cargo aircraft had an average age of 10.2 years. With deliveries of more Boeing 777-9s and Airbus A350-900s due between 2024 and 2034, this age is set to reduce.

During the Covid-19 pandemic, in 2020 and 2021, Emirates used some of its Airbus A380s, Boeing 777 passenger aircraft and Boeing 777F freighters to airlift cargo, including several tonnes of vaccines, all over the world. As the profitability of the freighter aircraft became clear, a US$1bn investment was made to acquire two new Boeing 777-F1Hs and to convert four Boeing 777-31HERs into cargo aircraft.

Between December 2021 and December 2022, Emirates made a loss of US$1.061bn but turned it around in 2023 to a record profit of US$2.88bn, with an 81 per cent increase in revenue to US$29.242bn. The company's relentless focus on delivering safe, top-quality services and customer-centric initiatives, have built trust and goodwill with travellers around the world.

From December 2022 to December 2023, the airline carried 43.6 million passengers and 1.8 million tonnes of cargo. As of December 2023, the airline has 261 aircraft, comprising ten Boeing 777-21HLRs, 123 Boeing 777-31HER/36NERs, 11 Boeing 777F1Hs, 116 Airbus A380-842/861s and an Airbus A319-115X corporate jet (which is used by Emirates Executive, a subsidiary of Emirates).

By 2040, the entire current fleet of passenger, cargo and corporate aircraft will have been retired and replaced with almost 400 aircraft. Of these, there is scheduled to be 60 Airbus A350-900/1000s, 35 Boeing 777-8s, 170 Boeing 777-9s, 20 Boeing 787-8s, 15 Boeing 787-10s and five Boeing 777Fs.

Emirates amplified the reach of its network by signing up 11 new codeshare and interline partners, including United Airlines and Air Canada in 2023. As a result, Emirates' customers can now travel seamlessly to more than 500 destinations.

In addition to 261 passenger, freighter and corporate aircraft in use by the airline and its cargo subsidiary (Emirates SkyCargo), the Emirates Group has a fleet of training aircraft that are used by its flight academy to train future pilots. Three Diamond DA42-VI twin-engine training aircraft were ordered in 2023 to strengthen the Emirates Flight Training Academy. The academy also operates 22 Cirrus SR22 G6 single-engine piston light training aircraft and five Embraer Phenom 100EV light training jets, as of December 2023.

Through its history, Emirates has operated 393 passenger and cargo aircraft. Of these, 266 are still owned or operated by the airline, including five A380s as a source of spare parts. In this book, the history and fate of each aircraft used by the airline and its subsidiaries is reviewed.

Since 18 May 2013, Emirates Executive has operated an Airbus A319-115X CJ (ACJ319). It can carry a maximum of 19 passengers. The aircraft has been chartered by UAE-based businesses for flights to Middle Eastern destinations. Officials from UAE as well as some members of the Dubai royal family have also chartered it. (Babak Taghvaee)

For primary or basic training of cadet pilots, Emirates Flight Academy operates 22 Cirrus SR22 G6 piston-engine aircraft with r/c A6-CTA to A6-CTV. (Sam Ghost)

After graduation from Cirrus SR22 aircraft and obtaining a private pilot license (PPL), pilot cadets train on three Diamond DA-42-VI twin-engined training aircraft with r/c A6-DAA, A6-DAB and A6-DAC. A6-DAA is landing at Corfu for refuelling en route to Dubai for delivery to Emirates on 25 May 2023. (Bernhard Jensch)

After multi-engine training on Diamond DA-42s, cadet pilots with a commercial pilot license (CPL) go on to train on five Phenom 100EV light jets. These have r/c A6-DWA to A6-DWE. A6-DWA is at Dubai Air Show 2023. (Charles Cunliffe)

Chapter 1

Retired Passenger Aircraft

Emirates' First Aircraft

In 1984, Gulf Air (an airline from Bahrain) began to reduce its flights to Dubai as it was concerned that it was providing regional feeder flights for other carriers that could be harmful to the young tourism industry in the UAE. Subsequently, Dubai's royal family created an airline that was required to operate independent of government subsidies, apart from the US$10m start up. The newly created airline made its first flight from Dubai to Karachi, Pakistan, and Mumbai, India, in October 1985.

In 1984, Sheikh Mohammed bin Rashid al Maktoum, then UAE Minister of Defence and a member of Dubai's progressive royal family, asked Sir Maurice Flanagan, then managing director of Dubai National Air Travel Agency (Dnata) who had previously been employed at British Airways, Gulf Air, and BOAC, to review the potential for starting up a new airline. By December that year, a comprehensive business plan was ready, and the name 'Emirates' was chosen for the new airline.

In March 1985, Flanagan was tasked with the ambitious mission of launching an airline in just five months with $10m seed funding. He was told that the airline had to 'look good, be good, and make

AP-BCD, a Boeing 737-340, was one of the first aircraft operated by Emirates and is in Dubai in 1986. Its second aircraft, an Airbus A300B4-203, is parked next to it. (Keith Heywood)

This A300B4-203 with r/c AP-BBM was the second aircraft wet-leased by Emirates from Pakistan International Airlines (PIA) from October 1985 until November 1988. It is at Dubai in 1986. (Christopher Redford)

money'. There would be no subsidies or protection under Dubai's open skies policy. In its first year, Emirates carried 260,000 passengers and 10,000 tonnes of freight. Gulf Air suffered a 56 per cent drop in profits during Emirates' first year of operations, and a loss the following year.

Pakistan International Airlines (PIA) played a large role in establishing Emirates by providing technical and administrative assistance to the new carrier as well as providing two of its aircraft. One of them was an Airbus A300B4-203 wide-body, twin-engine, twin-aisle passenger aircraft with registration code (r/c) AP-BBM and construction number (c/n) 64, which had been operated by PIA since August 1983. The second aircraft was a Boeing 737-340 narrow-body, twin-engine passenger aircraft with r/c AP-BCD (c/n 23297), operated by that airline since 21 June 1985.

Emirates began wet-leasing the two PIA aircraft in October 1985. On 25 October, Emirates operated its flights from Dubai to Karachi and Mumbai, using these two aircraft. AP-BBM was returned to PIA in November 1988 and was operated by the originating airline until 2006 when it was retired and scrapped. AP-BCD was returned to PIA in October 1987 and remained there until it was retired.

Boeing 727-200 Advanced Fleet: 1985–95

In its first five years of operations, the airline's network grew to 14 destinations. In its first year, in 1985, it flew to Dubai, Mumbai, Delhi and Karachi; in 1986, it added Amman, Colombo, Cairo and Dhaka; in 1987, it flew to Male, Frankfurt and Istanbul; in 1988, its flights to Damascus started; and in 1989, Jeddah and Kuwait were added to its schedule.

The original two aircraft did not have sufficient capacity to manage the demand for seats. Delivery of the airline's first new aircraft, an Airbus A310-304 with r/c A6-EKA, would not be until 1987. To add capacity, Dubai's royal family authorised the transfer of two aircraft from the Dubai Air Wing to Emirates. The two VIP aircraft were equipped with passenger seats before the start of their flights. As the airline's fleet was small at that time, the addition of these two former VIP aircraft would increase capacity.

The first was a Boeing 727-2M7 with r/c A6-HRR (c/n 21951), operated by the air wing from November 1980, and the second was a Boeing 727-264 with r/c A6-HMM (c/n 22982) operated from July 1982.

In addition, Emirates also operated a second-hand Boeing 727-2K5 with r/c A6-EMC (c/n 21852), hired on a dry-leasing contract from December 1989 to 30 June 1993, at which point it was returned to its lessor, Shannon Air Leasing.

As a T-tailed narrow-body airliner, the Boeing 727 was one of the most successful and best-selling passenger aircraft of the 1970s. Powered by Pratt & Whitney JT8D low-bypass turbofans, the Boeing 727-200 series operated by Emirates were stretched versions of the basic variants (Boeing 727-100). The 6.1m (20ft) increase in the aircraft's length was made possible by adding a 3m (10ft) fuselage section ('plug') ahead of the wings and another 3m (10ft) fuselage section behind them.

The Boeing 727-200 had an Advanced variant which, unlike the basic model, had a gross weight increased from 76,700 to 95,000kg (69,000 to 209,500lb). Production of the Boeing 727-200 Advanced began in 1972. In total, 310 Boeing 727-200s were manufactured between 1967 and 1972, and 935 Boeing 727-200 Advanced were manufactured between 1972 and 1984.

The Advanced version of the 727-200 had more powerful engines and an increased fuel capacity. Its maximum take-off weight (MTOW) was 84.3–95.3 tonnes (185,800–210,000lb). The Boeing 727-200 Advanced had an increased range from 1,930 to 2,550nmi (3,570 to 4,720km/2,220 to 2,930 miles) or by 32 per cent. All Boeing 727s operated by Emirates had JT8D-17R turbofan engines. Those on A6-EMB were equipped with hush-kits to reduce engine noise.

Emirates' two Boeing 727s were retired from service in May and October 1995. They were sold to the newly formed Qatar Airways. With that airline, A6-EMA became A7-ABC and was operated until 2001, while A6-EMB became A7-ABD and was operated until August 2000. Both airlines operated a three-seat cabin configuration for 20 first class seats and 114 economy seats.

Emirates operated its Boeing 727s across the same routes as the 737-340 leased from PIA. They flew daily services between Dubai and Karachi, Pakistan, and also from there to Amman, Jordan, and Cairo, Egypt. They also flew to Asian destinations including Colombo, Sri Lanka.

This Boeing 727-264 Advanced, formerly of the Dubai Air Wing, with r/c A6-HHM, was used by Dubai's royal family between July 1982 and July 1988. In use by Emirates, the aircraft was known as r/c A6-EMB. Here it is at Heathrow Airport, London, on 13 July 1985. (Paul Thallon)

Dubai Air Wing operated this Boeing 727-2M7 with r/c A6-HRR between November 1980 and December 1985. After its transfer to Emirates, it received r/c A6-EMA, and was operated until May 1996, when it was retired. It was then delivered to Qatar Airways where it became A7-ABC. Here, it is in its Dubai Air Wing colours prior to transfer to Emirates. (Carl Ford)

Boeing 727-264 with r/c A6-EMB is one of the three operated by Emirates. In October 1985, it was retired from Emirates and transferred to Qatar Airways, which operated it as A7-ABD until August 2000. It was retired again and sold to Pacific Aircorp, an aircraft leasing company, then converted to a freighter between 18 July 2001 when it was purchased and March 2002, when its conversion was complete. Astar Air Cargo leased it from November 2002 until July 2011 when Pacific Aircorp sold it to DHL. A year later, Kalitta Charters II bought it and put it into service. (EX/ZX collection)

Airbus A310-300 Fleet: 1987–2009

The first new aircraft Emirates bought was an Airbus A310-304 with r/c A6-EKA. It was delivered to the airline on 3 July 1987; following its first flight at Toulouse on 8 October 1986. In total, Emirates has operated seven different A310-300 passenger aircraft and three pure cargo variants. Its last example exited service in 2009. The first three were the A310-304, each equipped with a pair of General Electric CF6-80C2A2 turbofan engines, while the remainder, including the cargo versions, were all A310-308s. Six of these had more powerful CF6-80C2A8 turbofan engines.

The Airbus A310 was a shortened variant of the successful Airbus A300 wide-body, twin-jet passenger aircraft. It carried fewer passengers (a maximum of 265) and had an increased range, of 5,150nmi (9,540km/5,930 miles), compared with 2,900nmi (5,375km/3,340 miles) for the A300B4-200. The greater range enabled long-range flights including transatlantic routes. The A310-300 series had an increased maximum take-off weight. Its increase in range was provided by additional centre and horizontal stabiliser (trim-tank) fuel tanks.

The A310-300s were equipped with wingtip fences. These provided improved aerodynamic efficiency, which also helped to increase the maximum range of the aircraft. In addition, the A310-300 incorporated a computerised fuel distribution system, which allowed its flight control surfaces to be trimmed during the flight and helped optimise the aircraft's centre of gravity by transferring up to 5,000kg (11,000lb) of fuel in and out of the horizontal stabiliser tank.

The first two A310s that Emirates received were 304-series. The second was delivered on 24 July 1987 and received r/c A6-EKB. Both new aircraft had seating for 195 passengers (18 in business class and 177 in economy class). In the next A310s, the seating configuration changed to three classes carrying a total of 181 passengers (18 in first class, 32 in business class and 131 in economy).

As Emirates expanded its operations and increased its flights, more A310s entered service. At least two of these were operated under long-term dry-lease contract. The third aircraft was an A310-304 with c/n 545, which was delivered on 3 January 1992 and received r/c A6-EKG. It had been built following an order placed by Europe Aero Service but was not taken up. The next aircraft were all A310-308s with c/n 588, 597, 600, 658, 667 and 695 and were delivered between February 1992 and May 1995. With Emirates, they received r/c A6-EKI, A6-EKJ, A6-EKH, A6-EKK, A6-EKL and A6-EKP.

A seventh example, with c/n 573, belonging to International Lease Finance Corporation (ILFC) was leased from November 1994 and operated with r/c A6-EKN. Three second-hand A310-308 aircraft, with c/n 592, 622 and 646, built for Aeroflot, Russia's flag carrier, were procured and converted into Freighter (cargo) aircraft for Emirates. They were also delivered in November and December 2006 and received r/c A6-EFB, A6-EFC and A6-EFA respectively. Unlike the A310-200F, which was a newly built aircraft, all available A310-300Fs were second-hand.

Each 310-308F had capacity to carry 39,000kg (85,980lb) of freight over a distance of 5,950km (3,697 miles). The aircraft has a maximum payload of 40,600kg (89,507lb). The main cargo deck could hold up to 16 standard 2.24 x 3.17m (88 x 125in) pallets. The underfloor hold could carry either 14 LD3 containers, or three standard 2.24 x 3.17m (88 x 125in) pallets and six LD3 standard containers.

In March and June 2009, Emirates received its first Boeing 777F1H heavy cargo aircraft with c/n 766 and 788. These received r/c A6-EFD and A6-EFE. Prior to their receipt, the airline sold three Airbus A310-308Fs to Turkish cargo airline Kuzu Air. A6-EFA was the first to be delivered in October 2008, followed by A6-EFB on 1 December 2008. A6-EFC was delivered on 30 April 2009. With Kuzu Air, they received r/c TC-LER, TC-SGM and TC-VEL and were operated by the airline until 2009 when they were all delivered to another Turkish cargo airline ULS Airlines Cargo.

Emirates replaced its remaining ten A310-304/308s with Airbus A330-200s between 1997 and 2007. A6-EKA, the first A310 was retired two years before delivery of the first A330-200. It was sold to Airbus

Asset Management, a subsidiary of Airbus, which leased it to Royal Aviation, Canada 3000 Airlines and also Euroair between July 1997 and January 2004, when it was procured by Air Horizons and was operated by that company until the end of its life in 2007.

A6-EKB, A6-EKG, A6-EKH, A6-EKI, A6-EKJ, A6-EKN, A6-EKK, A6-EKL and A6-EKP were withdrawn from service by Emirates in November 2000, December 2000, May 2000, March 2001, May 2001, April 2002, May 2007, September 1999 and February 2002 respectively. Among them, A6-EKB was

A6-EKA is an Emirates A310-304, operated between July 1987 and May 1997. It was owned by Airbus Asset Management, which then leased it to various airlines until it was sold it to Air Horizons, which operated it between 2004 and 2007. A6-EKA is at Frankfurt Airport on 22 June 1991. (Mike Kell)

Emirates used this Airbus A310-304 from 1987 until 2000. Iran Air purchased it in November 2000 and operated it until 2019 when it was withdrawn from service following damage to its undercarriage during maintenance. It can be seen at Heathrow Airport, London, in 1995. (Christopher Redford)

Iran Air's A310-304 with r/c EP-IBL was once A6-EKB with Emirates. It was one of six wide-body passenger aircraft that Iran Air flew to Europe until 2019, when it was withdrawn from use. (Iran Air)

A6-EKN was an Emirates A310-304s. It is at Zürich Airport while carrying a Festival 1999 sticker on its fuselage in January of that year. (Martin Ortle)

In Zurich, in May 1998, is Emirates A310-308 with r/c A6-EKJ. It was retired then sold to Air Transat in May 2001. (Martin Ortle)

sold to Iran Air and operated with r/c EP-IBL until 2019, when it was withdrawn from service at Imam Khomeini International Airport, Tehran.

Air Transat, an airline from Canada, procured A6-EKG, A6-EKH, A6-EKI, A6-EKJ and A6-EKK after their retirement from Emirates' service, while A6-EKL and A6-EKP, which had been sold to Airbus, were sold on to Qatar Airways and Air India respectively. The A310-308 with r/c A6-EKN, which had been leased by Emirates from 1994 to 1999 was leased to Royal Jordanian Airlines from 1999 to 2006 and TAP Air Portugal by ILFC aircraft leasing company from 2006 to 2007. ILFC sold it to White Airways in 2006. As of December 2023, none of the Emirates' former A310s were airworthy.

Airbus A300B4-600R Fleet: 1989–2003

In total, Emirates has operated six different A300B4-600Rs, delivered between 1989 and 1995 and withdrawn from service between 1999 and 2003. A300B4-605R was one of two extended range variants of the A330B4-600 series of wide-body passenger aircraft. Emirates operated its A300B4-605Rs in conjunction with the fleet of its A310-304/308s for long-distance routes with high demand.

Airbus's first production aircraft, the A300, was the world's first twin-engine, double-aisle wide-body airliner. It entered mass production in 1971. One of the best and latest variants was the A300B4-600. It had many parts in common with the Airbus A310, and was a shorter version of it, entering mass production in 1981. A300B4-600 was slightly longer than the A300B2 and A300B4 variants. It had increased interior space enabling two additional rows of seats to be fitted.

A300B4-600 made its first flight on 8 July 1983. It was certified on 9 March 1984, and entered service with Saudi Arabian Airlines in June 1984. It incorporated the A310 cockpits, which featured digital technology and electronic displays, eliminating the need for a flight engineer. Since the Emirates' A310 and A300B4-600 pilots had a common type rating the pilot-training cost was reduced. All six in service with Emirates were extended range variants named A300B4-600R (R for range). With an additional trim fuel tank in the tail, the aircraft had slightly more range than the basic A300B4-600s. The A300B4-600R could carry a maximum 345 passengers and had a maximum range of 7,500km (4,050 nmi/4,700 miles).

The A300B4-605R was the most common extended-range variant in the family of A300B4-600 aircraft, which Emirates ordered alongside its A310-304/308s. Its six aircraft of this version had c/n 505, 558, 563, 608, 701 and 747. They first flew in Toulouse on 19 October 1988, 20 March 1990, 11 July 1990, 10 April 1991, 17 May 1993 and 2 December 1994 respectively. They were delivered to Emirates on 16 May 1988,

Emirates operated this Airbus A300B4-605R with r/c A6-EKD between 1990 and 2000. After its retirement, Tunisair procured it and operated it with r/c TS-IPA until January 2014 when it was withdrawn from use and put in storage. It is at Frankfurt on 21 June 1992. (Mike Kell)

This image, taken at Zürich Airport in May 2000, shows A6-EKM, an Emirates Airbus A300B4-605R sold to Lufthansa in 2003. It was sold to Mahan Air in 2010, which operated it until 2018 when it was leased to Iran Airtour. (M Ortle)

Formerly operated by Emirates as A6-EKM and Lufthansa as D-AIAZ, this A300B4-605R went on to Mahan Air in 2010. This aircraft with r/c EP-MNN is at Mehrabad Airport, Tehran, on 10 July 2011. (Babak Taghvaee)

This former Emirates A300B4-605R is operated by Iran's Mahan Air. EP-MNU was operated by Emirates as A6-EKF and then Lufthansa as D-AIAY. Mahan Air leased it to Iran Airtour in April 2021. (Babak Taghvaee)

11 June 1990, 24 September 1990, 14 June 1991, 31 August 1993 and 6 March 1995. In service with Emirates, they were operated with r/c A6-EKC, A6-EKD, A6-EKE, A6-EKF, A6-EKM and A6-EKO. Five had CF6-80C2-A1 turbofan engines while r/c A6-EKO had CF6-80C2-A5 engines. The A300B4-605Rs had cabin seating configurations for 216 passengers with 18 seats in first class, 35 in business class and 163 in economy.

The 29 A330-243s, which Emirates received brand new between 1999 and 2003, also took the place of the A300B4-605Rs. A6-EKC, A6-EKD, A6-EKE, A6-EKF, A6-EKM and A6-EKO exited the airline's fleet in August 1999, March 2000, February 2000, May 2001, April 2003 and April 2001 respectively. A6-EKC was sold to Airbus Asset Management; A6-EKD and A6-EKE went to Tunisair; A6-EKF and A6-EKM were sold to Lufthansa, while A6-EKO was sold to ILFC, which leased it to Middle East Airlines (Lebanon), Saudi Arabian Airlines and Onur Air. A6-EKF and A6-EKM became D-AIAY and D-AIAZ with Lufthansa and were operated until June and July 2009 respectively. Mahan Air purchased them via Kyrgyz Air and operated them in Iran with r/c EP-MNU and EP-MNN from 2009 and 2010 respectively. They were leased to Iran Airtour airline and flew with r/c EP-MDU and EP-MDN.

Airbus A330-200 Fleet: 1999–2016

Emirates operated Airbus A330-200 series twin-jet, wide-body and long-haul passenger aircraft as a replacement for its Airbus A310-304/308 and A300B4-605R wide-body passenger aircraft. In total, 29 different A330-243s entered service with Emirates between 1999 and 2003. They were withdrawn from service between 2010 and 2016. Among these, ten were owned by Emirates while the rest were operated under long-term dry-leasing contracts.

The Airbus A330 CEOs have three types, which are 200, 200F (freighter or cargo) and 300. The -300 series was slightly more popular than the -200 series. The A330-200 series had greater range and carried fewer passengers than the -300 series. It was selected by Emirates in the mid-1990s with deliveries starting from 1999.

The A330, as a passenger aircraft, dates back to the mid-1970s when Airbus began development of the A300B9, a larger derivative of the A300. It was a lengthened A300 with the same wing, coupled with the most powerful turbofan engine available at that time. It was developed to meet the growing need of airlines for wide-body passenger aircraft to fly the high-capacity, medium-range transcontinental routes and compete with the tri-engined McDonnell Douglas DC-10 and Lockheed L-1011 TriStar. These latter two had 25 per cent greater fuel consumption than the twin-engined aircraft.

While the A300B9 was scheduled to be a future medium-range replacement for A300B2s, a B11 variant was also developed to be a replacement for long-range A300B4s. It was designed to have four engines and later became the Airbus A340, an aircraft intended to replace narrow-body, long-haul Boeing 707s and Douglas DC-8s. Later, the B9 and B11 names for these two aircraft were changed to TA9 and TA11 (TA prefix for twin aisle), both capable of carrying a maximum of 410 passengers. With no funding available, the Airbus Supervisory Board approved the development of the TA9 as an A330 and the TA11 as an A340 on 27 January 1986. In that year, Airbus hoped five airlines would sign for both, and on 12 May sent sale proposals to the most likely candidates, including Lufthansa and Swissair.

On 12 March 1987, Airbus received the first orders for the twinjet. Domestic French airline Air Inter placed five firm orders and 15 options, while Thai Airways International requested eight aircraft, split evenly between firm orders and options. Design and development of the A330 alongside the A340 continued for four more years until production began on the first prototypes. The first A330 was complete on 14 October 1992, and took its maiden flight on 2 November.

With a weight of 181,840kg (401,000lb), including 20,980kg (46,300lb) of test equipment, it became the largest twin-engine passenger aircraft jet at that time. On 21 October 1993, the Airbus A330 received the European Joint Aviation Authorities (JAA) and the US Federal Aviation Administration (FAA) certifications after logging 1,114 hours of test flights in 426 cycles.

An A330 used for certification tests with Pratt & Whitney turbofan engines crashed, killing both test pilots and five Airbus employees on 30 June 1994. An investigation by the French Aviation Authority (Direction Générale d'Aviation) determined that the cause of the accident was a slow response and incorrect action of the crew during recovery while testing autopilot response during a one-engine-off, worst-case scenario, with the centre of gravity near its aft limit. As a result of that accident, the A330's operating procedures were revised.

The first Airbus A330ceo is the -300 series with a length of 63.69m (208ft 11in) and maximum range of 11,750km (6,340nmi; 7,300mi). It can carry 440 passengers. As of November 2023, a total of 784 A330-300 series aircraft were manufactured by Airbus, while 656 A330-200 passenger aircraft and 38 cargo variants had been manufactured and delivered. The A330-200, with a length of 58.82m (192.98ft) was shorter than the A330-300. However, it was also taller at 17.39m (57ft). Carrying 406 passengers, the A330-200 can fly a maximum 13,450km (7,260nmi/8,360 miles), which is slightly more than the maximum range of the A330-300.

To compensate for the smaller moment arm of the shorter fuselage, the vertical stabiliser height of the -200 was increased by 104cm (41in). This caused an increase in the height of the aircraft. In addition to the new vertical stabiliser, the A330-200 was equipped with new wings, which were strengthened allowing an increased maximum take-off weight of 229.8 tonnes (507,000lb). From the 2004 construction of the A330-200 with c/n 555, a new vertical stabiliser, which was 50cm (20in) shorter, became standard on the aircraft type. From 2009, production of a new version of the A330-200 named HGW (high gross weight) began. Korean Air was the first customer with an order for six in 2009.

Deliveries of A330s

In 1999, Emirates received its first five A330-243s, all equipped with Rolls-Royce Trent 772B-60 turbofan engines. The aircraft with c/n 248, 251, 283, 293 and 295 were delivered to Emirates on 30 March, 31 March, 7 July, 25 August and 22 September 1999 respectively. They received r/c A6-EKQ, A6-EKR, A6-EKS, A6-EKT and A6-EKU. All five belonged to DAE (Dubai Aerospace Enterprise) Capital, an aircraft leasing, maintenance, repair and overhaul company, and were operated by Emirates under long-term, dry-leasing contracts.

In 2000, eight more A330-243s were delivered with c/n 314, 316, 326, 328, 345, 348, 365 and 372 between 24 January and 21 December. They received r/c A6-EKV, A6-EKW, A6-EKX, A6-EKY, A6-EKZ, A6-EAA, A6-EAB and A6-EAC. Four were owned and four were operated under dry-leasing contracts. Of these, A6-EKX and A6-EKY were owned by DAE Capital and A6-EAA and A6-EAB were owned by BOC Aviation from Singapore.

In 2001, six aircraft with c/n 382, 384, 392, 396, 409 and 437 were delivered between 26 January and 26 November. They received r/c A6-EAD to A6-EAI. Three were owned by Emirates while three others were operated under long-term, dry-leasing contracts. They were A6-EAF, A6-EAG and A6-EAI all owned by DAE Capital.

Five more A330-243s were received in 2002, acquired under long-term leasing contracts. The aircraft with c/n 451, 452, 462, 491 and 494 were delivered on 29 January, 27 February, 12 March, 19 September and 13 September and received r/c A6-EAJ to A6-EAN respectively. The leasing companies included International Lease Finance Corporation (ILFC) and Babcock and Brown Aircraft Management (BBAM).

In 2003, the last five A330-243s were delivered to Emirates. Aircraft with c/n 455, 509, 518, 525 and 536 were delivered on 19 September, 7 March, 29 April, 2 April and 24 June 2003 respectively.

They received r/c A6-EAS, A6-EAO, A6-EAQ, A6-EAP and A6-EAR respectively. Among them, three were owned by Emirates while two, with r/c A6-EAO and A6-EAQ, were owned by Allco Aviation and Islamic Bank Consortium and were operated by Emirates under long-term leasing contracts.

Operation and Retirement of the A330s

Emirates equipped its A330-243s with two types of cabin configurations, one for 278 passengers (27 seats for business class and 251 for economy), and another for 237 passengers (12 first class, 42 business and 183 for economy). Nineteen of the Emirates A330-243s had first-class seats. The remaining ten had two-class seating configurations for high-demand routes and flew mostly to Asian destinations.

The Airbus A330 was designed for economic and affordable maintenance, like many other modern passenger aircraft of its era. The initial interval targets selected by the A330 Industry Steering Committee (ISC) for C and 2C checks covering power plant (engines and APU), systems and zonal tasks, were to escalate from 18mo/36mo to 24mo/48mo. These targets were not reached, owing to a lack of data at sufficiently high intervals. Check intervals were consequently cancelled in the A330 Maintenance Review Board Report (MRBR) Revision 13. Each former C or 2C interval task was then expressed in its most appropriate usage parameter(s): calendar time, flight-hours (FH), flight-cycles (FC), or a combination.

In February 2012, the first phase of C/2C-evolution was started in order to increase the intervals from 24 months or 10,000 flying hours to 42 months or 18,000 flying hours, but this was delayed. As expected,

Emirates operated this Airbus A330-243 with r/c A6-EAE between 31 January 2001 and 5 June 2015. It was scrapped for parts. It is at Dubai International Airport on 25 November 2014. (Babak Taghvaee)

the A330's maintenance costs did not reduce over time with the improvement of the C check procedures. This was a factor in the Emirates' decision to retire its young fleet of A330-243s by 2016.

A6-EAB, a leased aircraft, was the first to exit the fleet in December 2010. In 2011, A6-EAC and A6-EAL were returned to their lessors. A6-EAA (owned) and A6-EAN left the fleet in 2012. A6-EAA was procured by TAME (Linea Aerea del Ecuador), which operated it until 2019 when it was retired and scrapped. A6-EAI and A6-EAJ were retired and returned to their lessors in 2013.

Mass retirement of the remaining 21 took place. Eight (A6-EAD, A6-EAE, A6-EAG, A6-EAM, A6-EAO, A6-EAP, A6-EKQ and A6-EKW) were in 2015, and the rest (A6-EAF, A6-EAH, A6-EAK, A6-EAQ, A6-EAR, A6-EAS, A6-EKR, A6-EKS, A6-EKT, A6-EKU, A6-EKV, A6-EKX and A6-EKY) in 2016. Only two (r/c A6-EAD and A6-EAE) were scrapped after their retirement. They were flown from Dubai International Airport to Cornwall, UK, on 14 May and 5 June 2015 respectively.

In December 2023, nine of Emirates' original 29 A330-243s were still airworthy (A6-EKR, A6-EKZ, A6-EAJ, A6-EAS, A6-EAL, A6-EAO, A6-EAQ, A6-EAP and A6-EAR). Air Transat from Canada operates four of them (c/n 251, 455, 518 and 536, now with r/c C-GUFR, C-GUBH, C-GUBC and C-GUB). Three are owned, while C-GUBC is leased from Maleth-Aero. A6-EAK was the last A330-243 to be retired. Its last flight from Dubai to Trivandrum, India, and back to Dubai was logged on 29 October 2016. Emirates announced that the aircraft had flown nearly 45 million km over 60,000 hours.

On 14 February 2019, the airline announced it had reached an agreement with Airbus for a possible order for 40 A330-900 (A330 neo type) aircraft, and 30 A350-900 aircraft, in a letter of agreement signed with Airbus. The deal was worth US$ 21.4bn at list prices. When this book was written in December 2023, Emirates had not placed the order.

Emirates operated this A330-243 with r/c A6-EAH between 2001 and 2016. The aircraft was sold to Regiolease after its retirement. It is taking off from Dubai International Airport on 14 February 2015. (Babak Taghvaee)

This A330-243 with r/c A6-EAQ was used by Emirates between 29 April 2003 and 29 September 2016. It was sold to Airbus Financial Services in November 2016, which sold it to Maleth-Aero. Since 13 July 2017, Maleth-Aero has leased this aircraft to Air Transat, which is operating it with r/c C-GUBC. A6-EAQ can be seen seconds before landing at Imam Khomeini International Airport, Tehran, on 23 August 2013. (Babak Taghvaee)

This A330-243 with r/c A6-EAG was operated by Emirates between 6 April 2001 and 6 September 2015. After its retirement, the aircraft was procured by Avolon Aerospace on 16 November 2015 and leased to Hong Kong Airlines. It was impounded by the Hong Kong government in 2019 then was released and returned to Avolon Aerospace in 2020, which stored it in Dublin. This image shows it in Dubai in February 2015. (Babak Taghvaee)

Emirates operated this A330-243 with r/c A6-EAR between 2003 and 2016. After its retirement, the aircraft was sold to Airbus Company, which leased it to Air Transat with r/c C-GUBD between 2017 and 2020. It is in service with Emirates in Dubai in February 2015. (Babak Taghvaee)

This A330-243 with r/c A6-EAP was leased by Emirates from Hong Kong Aviation Capital between 2 April 2003 and 21 November 2015. It is landing at Larnaca, Cyprus, in August 2015. (Babak Taghvaee)

A6-EAH, an A330-243, was operated by Emirates between 22 June 2001 and 15 March 2016. It was sold to Regiolease, which leased it to Jordan Aviation from 2016 to 2022. It is at Dubai International Airport in February 2015. (Babak Taghvaee)

This Airbus A330-243 was operated by Emirates and is now in use by Air Transat. The aircraft with r/c C-GUBF (c/n 314) had r/c A6-EKV between 24 January 2000 and 9 July 2016. It is at Charles de Gaulle Airport, Paris, on 7 October 2023. (Babak Taghvaee)

This Air Transat A330-243 with r/c C-GUBH was operated by Emirates with r/c A6-EAS between 2003 and 2016. It is at Charles de Gaulle Airport, Paris, in June 2023. (Babak Taghvaee)

Airbus A340-300 Fleet: 2004–16

Emirates has operated 18 different Airbus A340 wide-body passenger aircraft. Despite being young, the A340s were soon retired from service due to their high fuel consumption. Airbus designed and produced the A340 in four main variants known as -200, -300, -500 and -600. Emirates operated eight -300s and ten -500s between 2003 and 2016.

The Airbus A340 design and development happened alongside that of the A330, mainly to replace the Airbus A300 wide-body passenger aircraft, the first aircraft designed and manufactured by Airbus. Initially named as Airbus A300B9 and B11, they were later redesignated as TA9 and TA11 (Twin Aisle 9 and 11). The first specifications of the TA9 and TA11 were released in 1982. Following a supervisory board meeting of Airbus Industrie in Munich, West Germany, on 27 January 1986, aircraft TA9 was officially named A330 and TA11, A340. The main difference between the aircraft was the number of engines. The A330 had two turbofan engines, the A340 was to have four.

In preparation for production of the A330 and A340, Airbus and its partners invested in new facilities in the UK and France. The A330 and A340 programmes were jointly launched on 5 June 1987. The first variant of the A340, the -200 prototype flew on 21 October 1991, marking the start of a 2,000-hour test flight programme involving six aircraft. On 2 February 1993, Lufthansa was the first airline to receive an A340-200, which was put into service on 15 March. A slightly stretched variant with better performance, characteristics and improved engines, the A340-300 was designed and developed, and the first aircraft of this type was delivered to Air France on 17 August 1993.

The A340-300 series aircraft could carry a maximum 375 passengers in economy cabin configuration or 250–290 passengers in a three-class cabin configuration. For the shorter A340-200 serie, these figures were 303 and 210–250. The A340-300 was 63.69m (208ft 11in) long, while the A340-200 series was 59.4m (195ft). Both models used CFM International CFM56-5C turbofans, however, the version fitted to the A340-200 produced a maximum thrust of 138.78kN (31,200lbf), while those on the A340-300 had a maximum thrust of 151.24kN (34,000lbf). With more powerful engines, the A340-300s had a maximum take-off weight of 276.5 tonnes (610,000lb) while the A340-200 series had a maximum of 275 tonnes (606,000lb).

Under a leasing contract, Emirates took eight A340-313s previously operated by Singapore Airlines from 2004. The aircraft belonged to Allco Aviation and had c/n 139, 149, 163, 166, 185, 190, 202 and 236. Singapore Airlines operated them with r/c 9V-SJD, 9V-SJE, 9V-SJG, 9V-SJH, 9V-SJI, 9V-SJJ, 9V-SJK and 9V-SJN between 1996 and 2003. Boeing Aircraft Holding Co purchased them and sold them to Allco Aviation. Deliveries took place on 25 March, 10 May, 30 January, 6 February, 8 March, 217 February, 14 April and 9 January 2004 respectively. They received r/c A6-ERS, A6-ERT, A6-ERO, A6-ERN, A6-ERP, A6-ERQ, A6-ERR and A6-ERM with Emirates.

These A340-313s had tri-class cabin configuration for 267 passengers including 12 first class seats, 42 business class and 213 economy class. They were used for European and Asian flights until they were retired between 2013 and 2016. With the delivery of more B777-300ERs, which were more profitable to operate, the A340s were gradually withdrawn from service.

The first four A340-313s, which were retired in 2013, were A6-ERQ, A6-ERR, A6-ERS and A6-ERT. They left Emirates on 16 January, 27 February, 4 February and 9 April 2013 respectively. A6-ERQ and A6-ERR were later purchased by HiFly Malta and were leased to various airlines with r/c CS-TQY and CS-TQZ until 2021 and 2022, when they were both put into storage at Beja International Airport,

A6-ERP was one of ten A340-313s operated by Emirates. It is landing at Dubai International Airport on 9 February 2015. After its retirement on 24 October 2016, Castlelake, an aircraft leasing company, sold it to HiFly Malta in 2017. (Babak Taghvaee)

This A340-313, with c/n 236, was operated by Singapore Airlines with r/c 9V-SJN between 20 September 1998 and 28 August 2003 when Boeing procured it. It was later sold to Castlelake, an aircraft leasing company, which leased it to Emirates between 9 January 2004 and 2 October 2016. It is at Frankfurt on 14 August 2016. (DUB Ramp)

A6-ERQ was another A340-313 that Emirates operated. It is taking off from Dubai International Airport in February 2015. (Babak Taghvaee)

This A340-313 was once operated by Emirates as A6-ERQ. It has been in use by HiFly Malta as 9H-TQY. It is at Charles de Gaulle Airport, Paris, on 22 August 2023. Just seven days after this image was taken, the aircraft was flown to Beja Airport, Portugal, to be stored and possibly scrapped. (Babak Taghvaee)

Portugal, with r/c 9H-TQY and 9H-TQZ. A6-ERS and A6-ERT were sold to Willis Air Lease after they left Emirates and were scrapped by Tarmac Aerosave in May and June 2013 respectively.

The remaining four A340-313s with r/c A6-ERO, A6-ERN, A6-ERP and A6-ERM left the fleet on 31 January, 29, 24 and 2 October 2016, respectively. The first two aircraft were purchased by AS Air Lease, which sold them to Tarmac Aerosave. That company scrapped them in 2017. The other two were purchased by HiFly Malta and received r/c 9H-FOX and 9H-JAI. They were leased to various airlines or were operated directly by the airline in 2023 and 2021 respectively. They were stored at Beja, Portugal, for parts and then to be scrapped.

Airbus A340-500 Fleet: 2003–16

The Airbus A340-500 has the longest range among the family of four-engined, wide-body passenger aircraft. When it was introduced, it had the longest range of all passenger aircraft. The prototype flew for the first time on 11 February 2002 and was certified on 3 December. Designed for ultra long-haul routes, the -500 has a range of 16,668km (9,000nmi/10,357 miles). It can travel non-stop from London to Perth, Western Australia, though a return flight requires a fuel stop due to headwinds. Air Canada was to be its launch customer. However, it declared bankruptcy in January 2003, making Emirates the launch customer. With this aircraft, the airline launched a non-stop service from Dubai to New York carrying 313 passengers in a three-class cabin layout across 16,020km (8650nmi/9,954 miles).

Compared to the A340-300, the -500 has a 4.3m (14.1ft) fuselage stretch, an enlarged and strengthened wing, a significant increase in fuel capacity (around 50 per cent larger than the -300), slightly higher cruising speed, a larger horizontal stabiliser and a larger vertical tailplane. The centreline main landing gear was changed to a four-wheel bogie to support the additional weight. The A340-500 is powered by four 240kN (54,000lbf) thrust Rolls-Royce Trent 553 turbofans and uses the Honeywell 331–600[A] APU. Named A340-541, it was equipped with Trent 553-61 variants while the A340-313s, which were all dry-leased, had four CFN56-5C4 turbofans, each producing 151kN (34,000lbf) thrust.

Emirates purchased ten A340-500 series aircraft and also planned to purchase the stretched variant known as A340-600. For Emirates, Airbus designed the A340-600HGW (high gross weight) version, which flew for the first time on 18 November 2005 and was certified on 14 April 2006. With a maximum take-off weight of 380 tonnes (840,000lb) and a range of up to 14,630km (7,900nmi/9,090 miles), the A340-600HGW was powered by four 61,900lbf (275kN) thrust Rolls-Royce Trent 560 turbofans. During the Paris Air Show 2003, Emirates ordered 18 A340-600HGWs but postponed the order and later cancelled it. Its rival, Qatar Airways became the sole buyer of the A340-600HGW variant with an order for four, which were delivered in 2006 and 2007.

The ten A340-541s that Emirates received had c/n 394, 457, 471, 485, 520, 572, 608, 611, 685 and 694. They received r/c A6-ERF, A6-ERA, A6-ERB, A6-ERC, A6-ERD, A6-ERE, A6-ERG, A6-ERH, A6-ERI and A6-ERJ and were delivered on 30 July 2004, 22 November 2003, 18 November 2003, 29 November 2003, 3 December 2003, 21 May 2004, 30 November 2004, 17 December 2004, 1 August 2005 and 29 September 2005 respectively. The late delivery of A6-ERF was due to it being used by Airbus Industrie for test flights as an A340-500 prototype. While a test aircraft, it had r/c F-WWAI and then F-WWTE. All ten A340-541s had tri-class cabin configuration for a total 258 passengers (12 first class, 42 business and 204 economy).

The A340-541s were withdrawn from service between 2013 and 2016. A6-ERF had accumulated more time and cycles than the rest so was the first to retire as it neared its D check time sooner than the rest. It was stored in Dubai Airport in May 2013, then flown to Ras Al Khaimah International Airport in August 2013, where it was scrapped.

A6-ERA retired on 14 November 2014 and was flown to Tarbes on 1 December. Universal Asset Management procured it in May 2019. A6-ERB, A6-ERC, A6-ERD, A6-ERE, A6-ERG, A6-ERH, A6-ERI and A6-ERJ were retired in 2014 and 2015. After several months of storage in Dubai they were flown to Tarbes. All were purchased by Airbus Financial Services to be sold or leased to other airlines. A6-ERH was sold to South African airline Global Aviation. A6-ERI and A6-ERJ were sold to AHS Aviation Services and Global Aviation respectively.

As of December 2023, A6-ERF, A6-ERA, A6-ERB, A6-ERC and A6-ERE had been scrapped while A6-ERD, A6-ERG, A6-ERH, A6-ERI and A6-ERJ were stored with r/c 2-RLBC, F-WTAZ, ZS-GAU, F-WTAY and 2-RLAV, 2-RLBC, 2-RLAV and ZS-GAU at O.R. Tambo International Airport, Johannesburg. F-WTAY was stored at Teruel Airport, Spain, while F-WTAZ was stored at Tarbes, awaiting sale.

Only one A340-541 with r/c A6-ERG had an accident while in service with Emirates. On 20 March 2009, the aircraft departed Melbourne for Dubai International Airport with flight number 407. It failed to take off properly and hit several structures at the end of the runway. Despite damage to its fuselage, it continued to climb. Its pilots declared an emergency and safely landed back in Melbourne a few minutes later after dumping its fuel.

The accident investigation was performed by the Australian Transport Safety Bureau (ATSB) and indicated that the captain and first officer made an error in judgement during take-off. Studies showed that the aircrew had difficulty recognising that incorrect data had been entered into its avionic equipment, resulting in poor take-off performance. A6-ERG was repaired and flown by Emirates for a number of years.

Model -541 had the greatest range among the family of A340 wide-body and long-haul passenger aircraft. Despite being superior in many aspects to other models, they were not popular on the second-hand market, A6-ERB being scrapped at Tarbes in April 2015 after finding no buyer. It is taking off from Dubai International Airport on 14 February 2015, just a month prior to its retirement. (Babak Taghvaee)

Emirates operated this Airbus A340-541 with r/c A6-ERH between December 2004 and October 2014. It is at Zurich on 30 January 2009. (DUB Ramp)

A6-ERD, one of Emirates' ten A340-541 ultra long-range, wide-body passenger aircraft, is at Zürich Airport in July 2007. The aircraft was operated between 3 December 2003 and 9 January 2015, when it was sold to Global Aviation. (M Ortle)

F-WTAZ was operated by Emirates as A6-ERG between 2004 and 2014 and has been stored in Tarbes for years. It was photographed there in December 2023. (Babak Taghvaee)

Chapter 2

Current Fleet of Passenger Aircraft

Boeing 777-200 Fleet: 1996–Today

The Boeing 777 is one of the best-selling wide-body passenger aircraft ever manufactured. Emirates is the largest operator of the aircraft with 139 of them in three types in service as of December 2023. Its fleet includes nine Boeing 777-200ER series, 119 -300ER series and 11 -200F cargo. The -200 series and their Extended Range (ER) variants are the oldest still in service and are planned to be retired and replaced with modern Boeing 777-9s. Eleven were under construction in the US as of December 2023.

Two models of Boeing 777s were designed and built and differed in terms of fuselage length and range. The first was the Boeing 777-200 series, the prototype of which had its maiden flight on 12 June 1994. United Airlines became the first recipient of the type on 15 May 1995 when a Boeing 777-222 with c/n 26916 was delivered; it is still airworthy today as N777UA.

With a 247-tonne (545,000lb) maximum take-off weight and two engines each producing a maximum thrust of 340kN (77,000lbf), it has a range of 5,240nmi (9,700km/6,030 miles), seating 305 passengers in a three-class configuration. The -200 was primarily aimed at US domestic airlines, although several others from Asia and Europe procured it, including Emirates. In total, 88 Boeing 777-200s were manufactured and delivered to nine different customers; of these, 55 were in service in 2018, and 21 (including 11 cargo variants) as of December 2023.

In 1992, Emirates ordered seven Boeing 777s and had an option to buy seven more. This Boeing 777 procurement signalled the airline's ambition and was a vote of confidence for the industry, which had been hit by the negative consequences of the first Persian Gulf War in 1991.

The first three of these were model -21Hs with c/n 27247, 27248 and 27249. These aircraft logged their first flights in the US on 2 May, 14 June and 25 September 1996 respectively. They received r/c A6-EMD, A6-EME and A6-EMF and were delivered to Emirates on 5 June, 3 July and 16 October 1996. Each was equipped with a pair of Rolls-Royce Trent 877-17 turbofan engines with a take-off thrust of 351.0kN (78,910lbf).

The next four, delivered in 1997, were all ER variants classified Boeing 777-21HER. The aircraft with c/n 27250, 27251, 27252 and 27253 received r/c A6-EMI, A6-EMH, A6-EMG and A6-EMJ and were delivered on 25 July, 15 May, 11 April and 30 September 1997 respectively.

Initially known as Boeing 777-200IGW (increased gross weight), the Extended Range Boeing 777-200 variant has additional fuel capacity and an increased maximum take-off weight of 298 tonnes (658,000lb) and a 13,084km (7,065nmi/8,130 miles) range. While the Boeing 777-200 competed with the Airbus A330-300 market, the Boeing 777-200ER competed with the Airbus A340-300. Emirates received six Boeing 777-21HERs, each fitted with a pair of Rolls-Royce RB211 Trent 892-17 (Trent 892-17) turbofan engines (406.8kN/91,450lbf) take-off thrust).

In 1998, Emirates received two more Boeing 777-21HERs increasing its total to nine. The last two extended range 777s were A6-EMK and A6-EML with c/n 29324 and 29325. They were delivered on 30 October and 25 November 1998 respectively. While the Boeing 777-21Hs had seats for 346 passengers (42 for business class and 304 for economy), the Boeing 777-21HERs had 274 seats in three classes (12 first class, 42 business and 220 economy).

Between 2007 and 2009, Emirates took delivery of ten Boeing 777-21HLRs, a long-range variant of the Boeing 777-200 model. Named Worldliner by Boeing, this variant was designed to be one of the longest-range commercial airliners when it entered service in 2006. With a maximum design range of 8,55nmi (15,844km/9,845 miles), it holds the world record for the longest non-stop flight by a commercial airliner. It was designed to meet the needs of various airlines.

Development of the Boeing 777-200LR variant occurred at the same time as that of the Boeing 777-300ER, the extended range variant of the stretched 777-300 series. Like the Boeing 777-300ER, the -200LR had an increased maximum take-off weight and three optional auxiliary fuel tanks in the rear cargo hold. In addition, it had 12⅘ft (3.9m) extended raked wingtips, redesigned main landing gear, and additional structural strengthening. Twelve -200LR customers took delivery of 61 aircraft. Pakistan International Airlines was the first on 26 February 2006, while Emirates received the largest number with ten, delivered between 2007 and 2009.

The first three, with c/n 35572, 35573 and 35576, (r/c A6-EWA, A6-EWB and A6-EWC) were delivered on 31 August, 21 September and 19 November 2007 respectively. Five more, with c/n 35577, 35578, 35582, 35586 and 35587 were delivered with r/c A6-EWD to A6-EWH respectively, between 25 January and 23 December 2008. The last two, with c/n 35589 and 35590, were delivered as A6-EWI and A6-EWJ on 26 January and 30 March 2009.

The Boeing 777-21HLRs were equipped with General Electric GE90-110B1 engines, each with take-off thrust of 492.7kN (110,760lbf). With these engines, they had the highest maximum take-off weight of all the Boeing 777-200 variants in service with Emirates, at 347,452kg (766,000lb). Boeing 777-21HLRs were equipped with 302 seats including 38 for business class and 264 for economy.

Between 2014 and 2016, Emirates retired its three Boeing 777-21Hs and six Boeing 777-21HERs. Boeing 777-21H A6-EMD and A6-EME were retired in 2014. They were procured by Universal Asset Management Inc based in Memphis, and were scrapped a year later. The third Boeing 777-21H with A6-EMF was retired on 14 July 2015 when it was flown from Dubai to Pinal Airpark, Arizona, where it was scrapped.

A6-EMF was one of the first three Boeing 777s operated by Emirates. The Boeing 777-21H was in service between 16 October 1996 and 14 July 2015. It is seen here a few months prior to its retirement at Dubai on 15 February 2015. (Babak Taghvaee)

The six Boeing 777-21HERs were all retired in 2016. A6-EMK was procured by Air Peace; the remaining five by a Russian airline VIM Avia. VIM Avia operated them until 2017. Three were later sold to Russian airline Red Wings and two were scrapped. As of December 2023, Red Wings operated them with r/c RA-73329, RA-73330 and RA-73331 for flights to Egypt, Thailand and Sri Lanka. They were previously A6-EMI, A6-EMH and A6-EML in Emirates' service.

In December 2023, A6-EWH, one of the ten Boeing 777-21HLRs, was in storage while the rest were airworthy. They flew to Amman, Ahmedabad, Baghdad, Bahrain, Barcelona, Basra, Bengaluru, Buenos Aires, Cochin, Dammam, Dar-es-Salaam, Istanbul, Kuwait City, Lyon, Mexico City, Montreal, Mumbai, Tehran, Venice and Rio de Janeiro.

This Boeing 777-21HER with r/c A6-EMH is equipped with a pair of Rolls-Royce Trent 892 turbofan engines and was operated by Emirates between 15 May 1997 and 27 April 2016. After its retirement, it was sold to Russian airline VIM Avia and was still airworthy with Red Wings airline as RA-73330 in December 2023. It is in Dubai in February 2015. (Babak Taghvaee)

A6-EMI, a Boeing 777-21HER operated between 1997 and 2016 by Emirates, was sold to VIM Avia and is now in use by Red Wings. The aircraft is at Dubai on 14 February 2015. (Babak Taghvaee)

This Boeing 777-21HER with r/c A6-EMJ was operated by Emirates between September 1997 and October 2016. It was sold to RegioLease, which leased it to VIM Avia between April and October 2017. It was scrapped in January 2020. Here it is at Dubai International Airport on 18 February 2015. (Babak Taghvaee)

In total, Emirates operated six different Boeing 777-21HERs. A6-EMK was one of them. It was operated between 30 October 1998 and 15 January 2017. After its retirement, it was purchased by Air Peace and as of December 2023, it was still airworthy as 5N-BVE. (Babak Taghvaee)

Emirates operates ten Boeing 777-21HLRs including this with r/c A6-EWC, in Dubai in February 2015. It has been in use by Emirates since 19 November 2007. (Babak Taghvaee)

A6-EWG is another GE90-110B1 turbofan engine-equipped Boeing 777-21HLR in use by Emirates since 19 November 2007. (Babak Taghvaee)

This Boeing 777-21HLR with r/c A6-EWJ has been in use by Emirates since 30 March 2009. It is a frequent flier to Tehran, where it was photographed on 30 October 2021. (Mike H)

All Emirates' Boeing 777-21HLRs have C38Y264 seating configuration. This image shows business class seats. (Emirates)

This image shows economy seats in an Emirates' Boeing 777-21HLR. (Emirates)

Boeing 777-300 Fleet: 1999–Today

Emirates is the world's largest operator of Boeing 777 passenger aircraft, the majority of which are -300 series. The airline has operated 135 Boeing 777-300 series passenger aircraft in two variants, the basic and extended range. As of December 2023, 123 examples, all extended range, are still in use. Those built to the airline's specification are 777-31HER. The fleet includes those classified Boeing 777-36NER, which were built for GE Capital Aviation Services and operated by Emirates under long-term leasing contracts. The airline's 12 Boeing 777-31Hs and 23 Boeing 777-31HER/36NERs were retired between 2016 and 2022.

The Boeing 777-300 series is the second member of the Boeing 777 family and the stretched variant of Boeing 777 wide-body passenger aircraft. Its production started in 1996, with the major assembly of the first aircraft of this type commencing between March and July 1997. The first prototype rolled out on 8 September. The 10.1m (33ft) stretching of the Boeing 777-300 is created by adding 5.3m (17ft) in ten frames forward and 4.8m (16ft) in nine frames aft for a 73.8m (242ft) length.

As the Boeing 777-300 fuselage was extended by 20 per cent, it could house 60 extra seats in a tri-class cabin configuration for a total 370 passengers, or 75 additional seats in a two-class cabin configuration for 451 passengers. In all-economy cabin configuration, it could carry a maximum 550 passengers. The Boeing 777-300 model has 171,200-litre (45,200-gallon) fuel capacity and with a pair of turbofan engines each producing 84,000–98,000lbf (374–436kN) take-off thrust, it has a 263.3–299.6 tonne (580,000–661,000lb) maximum take-off weight (depending on engine type).

Emirates has operated 12 Boeing 777-31Hs. They were delivered between November 1999 and June 2003 and were withdrawn from service between July 2016 and October 2018. They were equipped with 364 seats in tri-class cabin configuration for 12 first class seats, 42 business class and 310 economy class.

Owned by Singapore Aircraft Leasing, this Boeing 777-31H, with r/c A6-EMN, was operated by Emirates under a long-term leasing contract between 23 December 1999 and 28 August 2017. It is at Dubai International Airport on 18 February 2015. (Babak Taghvaee)

Owned by ILFC, this Boeing 777-31H with r/c A6-EMR was operated by Emirates between 19 May 2002 and 11 March 2018. From 3 September 2018, it has been in use by Cathay Pacific with r/c B-HNS. It is in Dubai on 13 February 2015. (Babak Taghvaee)

This Trent 895 turbofan engine-equipped Boeing 777-31H, with r/c A6-EMS, was operated by Emirates between 2002 and 2017. Since 2022, Jordan Aviation has leased it from BOC Aviation Aircraft Leasing Company. It is in Dubai in February 2015. (Babak Taghvaee)

The first two, with c/n 29062 and 29063, were delivered to Emirates with r/c A6-EMM and A6-EMN. They were owned by Singapore Aircraft Leasing (SALE) and operated under a long-term leasing contract.

A third Boeing 777-31H with c/n 28680 was delivered to Emirates on 26 September 2000. With r/c A6-EMO, the aircraft was owned by International Lease Finance Corporation (ILFC) and was operated under a long-term leasing contract.

On 22 March 2001, A6-EMP, the fourth Boeing 777-31H, was delivered. It was also owned by ILFC and operated under a long-term leasing contract. Five more with r/c A6-EMQ, A6-EMR, A6-EMS, A6-EMT and A6-EMU were delivered on 24 April, 19 May, 2 July, 3 September and 30 September 2002 respectively. They were first flown on 1 April, 2 May, 2 July, 3 and 21 September 2002 respectively. A6-EMQ, A6-EMR and A6-EMT were owned by ILFC, while the rest were owned by SALE.

All Emirates' Boeing 777-31Hs were retired from service and were returned to their lessors between 2016 and 2018. A6-EMO was retired in 2016. In 2017, A6-EMM, A6-EMN, A6-EMP, A6-EMS and A6-EMU exited the fleet, while in 2018, the remaining aircraft left the fleet and returned to their lessors. A6-EMW was written off following a landing incident at Dubai International Airport. The aircraft burned although all 282 passengers and 18 crew exited safely.

The Extended Range Boeing 777-300s

The Extended Range variant of the Boeing 777-300 is one of the most popular in the market. In total, 146 have been or are operated by Emirates. Of these, 23 had exited the fleet as of December 2023. The Boeing 777-300ER has a higher maximum take-off weight and increased fuel capacity enabling a maximum range of 7,370nmi (13,650km/8,480 miles) with 396 passengers in a two-class seating arrangement.

The Boeing 777-300ER has raked and extended wingtips, a strengthened fuselage, wings with an aspect ratio of 9.0 and a modified main landing gear. The aircraft has a pair of General Electric GE90-115B turbofans, each producing 115,540lbf (513.9kN) take-off thrust, which makes it the most powerful jet engine in the world.

With two fuel-efficient engines, the Boeing 777-300ER became a primary driver of the twinjet's sales in the market of wide-body passenger aircraft. Its sales surpassed those of the Airbus A340 but also those of the Airbus A330ceo (conventional engine option). The Boeing 777-300ER has a typical operating cost advantage of around 8–9 per cent, representing a 20 per cent less fuel burn, over the A340-600. Boeing 777-300ERs have replaced Airbus A340s in many airlines, and have been purchased as replacements for Boeing 747-400s.

With an operating cost of US$44 per seat per hour, compared to an Airbus A380 at US$50 per seat per hour and US$90 per seat per hour for a Boeing 747-400 (2015 costs), the Boeing 777-300ER was also widely purchased as their replacements. Air France became the first to receive and operate the Boeing 777-300ER series, while Emirates became the largest operator. The aircraft became the best seller of its kind with 832 orders and deliveries as of 2023.

In 2005, Emirates made history with an order for 42 Boeing 777s valued at US$9.7 billion. It was the largest Boeing 777 order at that time, turning the airline into its largest operator in just a few years. Many of the orders were for -300ER variants, which were delivered by Emirates as Boeing 777-31HER between 2005 and 2007. Many were owned by ILFC and GECAS and were operated under long-term leasing contracts. Those from GECAS were known as Boeing 777-36NER.

In 2005, Emirates received ten Boeing 777-300ERs. They received r/c A6-EBA, A6-EBB, A6-EBC, A6-EBD, A6-EBE, A6-EBF, A6-EBG, A6-EBH, A6-EBI and A6-EBJ, with their deliveries taking place on 27 March, 30 March, 19 April, 16 May, 30 August, 2 November (two aircraft), 25 October, 1 December, 6 December, 23 November and 21 December respectively. Among these, A6-EBE, A6-EBG, A6-EBI and A6-EBJ were Boeing 777-36NERs originally ordered by GECAS for Emirates, while the rest were Boeing 777-31HERs ordered by ILFC, or were owned by the leasing company when they were operated by Emirates under long-term leasing contract.

In 2006, Emirates received 13 more Boeing 777-300ERs with r/c A6-EBK to A6-EBW. Among these A6-EBN, A6-EBO, A6-EBY, A6-EBQ and A6-EBW were B777-36NERs while the rest were B777-31HERs. A6-EBL and A6-EBP were owned by IFLC; A6-EBN was owned by GECAS; and A6-EBO, A6-EBQ and A6-EBW were owned by AerCap Holdings NV. Eight more Boeing 777-300ERs with r/c A6-EBX to A6-EBZ and A6-ECA to A6-ECE were delivered in 2007. Among these A6-EBY, A6-ECA, A6-ECC and A6-ECD were B777-36NERs and the rest were B777-31HERs. A6-EBX and A6-EBZ were owned by ILFC while A6-EBY and A6-ECA, A6-ECC and A6-ECD were owned by AerCap Holdings NV. A6-ECB was the only aircraft among these to be completely owned by the airline.

In 2008, Emirates received seven more B777-300ERs with r/c A6-ECF to A6-ECL while in 2009, 12 others with r/c A6-ECM to A6-ECX were delivered. Among these, A6-ECL, A6-ECM, A6-ECN, A6-ECO and A6-ECP were B777-36NERs, while the rest were B777-31HERs. Most of these aircraft were owned by Emirates. A6-ECL, A6-ECN and A6-ECP were owned by GECAS while A6-ECO was owned by AerCap Holdings NV and A6-ECR was owned by Doric Asset Finance.

In 2010, Emirates received three B777-300ERs with r/c A6-ECY, A6-ECZ and A6-EGA. Eleven more, with r/c A6-EGB to A6-EGL, were delivered in 2011; 12 more with r/c A6-EGM to A6-EGZ and A6-ENA to A6-END were delivered in 2012; and eight more with r/c A6-ENE to A6-ENL in 2013. This increased the total number of the B777-300ERs to 84. The acquisitions enabled the airline to expand its network, increase its flights and significantly increase its profitability. With this expanded fleet, the airline became the largest in the Middle East. All of these aircraft were B777-31HER and all were owned by Emirates.

Emirates received 12 more B777-31HERs with r/c A6-ENM to A6-ENX in 2014. Ten more were delivered in 2015, and received r/c A6-ENY and A6-ENZ and A6-EPA to A6-EPH. In 2016, 16 more, with r/c A6-EPI to A6-EPX were delivered. In 2017, 12 more with r/c A6-EPY, A6-EPZ and A6-EQA to A6-EQJ were delivered, followed by the last six with r/c A6-EQK to A6-EQP in 2018.

Deliveries of the last B777-31HERs to the airline enabled it to retire some of the first B777-31HERs and B777-36NERs. In March 2017, A6-EBD exited the fleet and returned to its lessor while in January 2018, A6-EBA and A6-EBL left the fleet. A6-EBP, A6-EBS, A6-EBT and A6-EBV also left the fleet in April, July, August and September 2018 respectively. In 2019, five more aircraft left Emirates and returned to their lessors, including A6-EBF (March), A6-EBH (June), A6-EBX (January), A6-EBZ (February) and A6-ECB (May).

In 2020, eight more B777-300ERs left Emirates including A6-EBB, A6-EBC A6-EBE, A6-EBG, A6-EBI, A6-EBJ, A6-ECL and A6-ECN and were returned to their lessors. In January and February 2021, A6-ECP and A6-EBN were returned to GECAS, while in September 2021, A6-EBO was returned to AerCap Holding Ltd.

Boeing 777-300ER Fleet Today

As of December 2023, Emirates had 123 B777-300ERs in its service. Among these, five were stored and 118 were airworthy. The average age of the fleet as of December 2023 was 10.8 years.

Fifty-three were configured with eight first-class seats, 42 business class and 310 economy seats. Thirty-two B777-300ERs had eight first-class seats, 42 business and 304 economy seats. Seventeen more had a two-class cabin configuration for 42 business class and 386 economy class seats. Twelve B777-300ERs delivered in 2016 and 2017 had eight first class, 42 business class and 306 economy seats. The last eight B777-300ERs had six first class, 42 business class and 306 economy seats.

In 2023, Emirates launched a programme for retrofitting the cabins of its Boeing 777s and A380s. By the end of 2025, Emirates will have installed almost 4,000 new premium economy seats, refurbished 728 first-class suites and upgraded more than 5,000 business class seats in 53 B777-300ERs and 67 Airbus A380s.

Since 21 October 2011, this Boeing 777-31HER with r/c A6-EGH has been in use by Emirates. This aircraft was damaged due to a ground collision with an A330-243 of Air Transat with r/c C-GUBL at Miami International Airport on 13 April 2023. It was repaired on 16 July 2023. It is landing at Larnaca on 17 April 2019. (Babak Taghvaee)

A6-ENG is a Boeing 777-31HER in use by Emirates. It was delivered on 29 February 2013. The aircraft is landing at Larnaca on 20 July 2018. (Babak Taghvaee)

Emirates has been using this Boeing 777-31HER with r/c A6-EPS since 29 September 2016. It is taking off from Larnaca on 8 May 2018. (Babak Taghvaee)

Emirates has been using this Boeing 777-31HER with r/c A6-EGW since 10 August 2012. This aircraft, which has a pair of GE90-115B turbofan engines, is landing at Larnaca on 19 July 2017. (Babak Taghvaee)

This Boeing 777-31HER, with r/c A6-ENU, has been operated by Emirates since 29 September 2014. It was put into storage at Al-Maktoum International Airport, Dubai, between 1 March and 8 June 2018, but returned to service later. It is landing at Larnaca on 8 August 2018. (Babak Taghvaee)

A6-ENK is an Emirates Boeing 777-31HER operated from 25 July 2013. It is performing a low pass over Larnaca on 30 August 2018. (Babak Taghvaee)

A6-ENF, a Boeing 777-31HER, first flew in the US on 22 January 2013 and was delivered on 31 January. It is at Khomeini International Airport, Tehran, on 1 October 2023. (Mike H)

On the 50th anniversary of the formation of the United Arab Emirates, the airline branded its aircraft with '50 United Arab Emirates'. This Boeing 777-31HER, with r/c A6-EPB, is at Khomeini International Airport, Tehran, on 14 November 2022. (Mike H)

A6-EPP is a Boeing 777-31HER with r/c A6-EPP, operated by Emirates since 29 July 2016. It received a 'Year of Zayed 2018' special livery in November 2017. It is at Mashhad International Airport, northeast Iran, on 24 October 2017. (Ata Tavanaee)

Larnaca, May 2023; A6-EGQ is an Emirates Boeing 777-31HER. (Babak Taghvaee)

This image, taken at Athens International Airport, shows an Emirates Boeing 777-31HER with r/c A6-ENX on 18 May 2023. (Babak Taghvaee)

First flown on 3 July 2014, this Boeing 777-31HER has been in use by Emirates since 29 July. It is landing at Dubai International Airport on 14 February 2015. (Babak Taghvaee)

Built at Boeing Everett (Seattle), this Boeing 777-31HER first flew on 27 April 2017 and was delivered to Emirates on 30 May. It is at Athens International Airport on 18 May 2023. (Babak Taghvaee)

This Boeing 777-31HER, with r/c A6-ENE, has been in use by Emirates since 23 January 2013. It is taking off from Dubai International Airport on 14 February 2015. (Babak Taghvaee)

A6-EQC, an Emirates Boeing 777-31HER, is landing at Athens. (Babak Taghvaee)

Boeing 777-31HER with r/c A6-ENT is taking off from Dubai International Airport in February 2015. This aircraft has been operated by Emirates since 15 August 2014. (Babak Taghvaee)

Another image of A6-ENG at Dubai International Airport while being pushed back before a flight on 18 February 2015. (Babak Taghvaee)

A6-EGD, a Boeing 777-31HER, at Dubai International Airport on 18 February 2015. (Babak Taghvaee)

Owned by AerCap Holdings NV, this Boeing 777-36NER has been in service since 29 November 2006. It is landing at Larnaca on 17 April 2019. (Babak Taghvaee)

This aircraft, which belongs to GECAS, was leased by Emirates between 16 December 2008 and 4 October 2020. Investment firm Dr. Peters Group purchased the aircraft and stored it at McConnell Air Force Base for conversion to a freighter aircraft on 2 September 2021. It is at Dubai International Airport on 15 February 2015. (Babak Taghvaee)

This Boeing 777-36NER belongs to AerCap Holdings NV and has been leased by Emirates since 7 May 2007. (Babak Taghvaee)

Those Boeing 777-300ERs with a tri-cabin class seating configuration have eight first-class suites in the front of the aircraft. This image shows one of them. (Emirates)

All of the Boeing 777-300ERs have 60 business seats. (Emirates)

Boeing 777-31HER with r/c A6-EGZ illustrating economy seats. (Babak Taghvaee)

The lighting in the cabin of A6-EGP, a Boeing 777-31HER. (Babak Taghvaee)

Boeing 777X Fleet: 2025–Future

In July 2014, Emirates, the launch customer for the latest and most modern variant of Boeing 777 known as the B777X series, finalised its order for 150 aircraft comprising 115 B777-91Hs and 35 shorter B777-81Hs. Four years later, the Emirates order was reduced, due to difficulties in financing its procurement. The total order decreased from 150 to 115 aircraft, comprising 85 B777-91Hs and 30 B777-81Hs. Despite the decrease, the airline remained the largest buyer of the aircraft. At the Dubai Air Show 2023, Emirates ordered an additional 90 B777Xs, consisting of 55 B777-91Hs and 35 B777-81Hs.

Boeing 777X is the latest series of the long-haul, wide-body, twin-engine jetliner, which is equipped with new General Electric GE9X turbofan engines, new composite wings with folding wingtips, greater cabin width and seating capacity, and more importantly, the technologies of the Boeing 787 Dreamliner, a game-changing contemporary passenger aircraft. Development of the Boeing 777X with two variants, known as B777-8 and B777-9, commenced in November 2013. The B777-8 has seating for a maximum 384 passengers and a range of 8,745nmi (16,196km/10,064 miles), while the B777-9 has seating for 426 passengers and a range of more than 7,285nmi (13,492km/8,383 miles).

Boeing 777-9X stretched the 777-300ER by four frames to 76.48m (250ft 11in) long, for a 344-tonne (759,000lb) maximum take-off weight to compete with the Airbus A350-1000, while the smaller Boeing 777-8X proposed stretching the 777-200ER by ten frames to 69.55m (228ft 2in), with a maximum take-off weight of 315 tonnes (694,000lb) and 88,000lbf (390kN) turbofans to compete with the A350-900.

On 23 October 2017, Boeing launched production of the Boeing 777-9 with the wing spar drilling. Completion of the first prototype was scheduled to take place in the first quarter of 2019. The B777X prototype was equipped with GE9X engines. A design flaw caused delays to the first flight of the aircraft.

By mid-November, flight-compliant engines were installed on the 777-9 prototype. After several successful ground tests, the aircraft's first flight from Paine Field in Everett lasted three hours and

The prototype Boeing 777-9, with c/n 64240 and r/c N779XW, rolled out of the factory on 25 January 2019 and flew on 25 January 2020. Since then, it has been extensively used for test flights. (Babak Taghvaee)

The Boeing 777X has a new longer composite wing with folding wingtips made by Liebherr Aerospace, which will significantly reduce fuel consumption compared to the Boeing 777-300ER. (Babak Taghvaee)

52 minutes. The second B777X prototype flew for the first time on 30 April 2020. Due to delays in the type certification tests, deliveries of the first B777s to customers were postponed until 2025.

As of December 2023, 13 Boeing 777Xs under production at Boeing Everett (Seattle) facility were for Emirates. They were all Boeing 777-91Hs, which are to be equipped with a pair of GE9X-105B1A turbofans each producing 110,000lbf (489.3kN) take-off thrust. The B777-9s earmarked for delivery to Emirates in 2025 have c/n 1605, 1611, 1615, 1620, 1624, 1642, 1647, 1651, 1659, 1668, 1682, 1688 and 1716. The first seven have already received Emirates r/c, which are A6-EZD, A6-EZT, A6-EZM, A6-EZA, A6-EZB, A6-EZQ and A6-EZS. Production of these aircraft started in 2019 and 2020.

Complementing Boeing 777Xs with Boeing 787 Dreamliners

According to plans, Emirates will replace its 123 Boeing 777-31HER/36NERs and a selection of Airbus A380s between 2025 and 2032. In addition, 35 Boeing 787-81H/101Hs will be operated as a replacement for ten Boeing 777-21HLRs currently in service, together with 29 A330-243s, which the airline retired between 2010 and 2016. Emirates once intended to procure the Airbus A330neo as a replacement for its retired A330-243s. However, the plans changed and the American rival, Boeing's 787 Dreamliner, was selected. The Dreamliner is a wide-body, twin-engined passenger aircraft, a successor of the Boeing 767 and a competitor of Airbus's A330neo and A350.

Initially, the Boeing 787 was designed to have two variants, the -8 and its stretched -9. Studies were conducted by Boeing to develop another stretched variant known as 787-10 at the request of Emirates and Qantas. The Boeing 787-10 could carry a maximum 310 passengers – 20 more than the Boeing 787-9. This variant would carry similar capacity to the Airbus A350-900, the Boeing 777-200ER, as well as the Boeing 777-200LR.

The Boeing 787-10 development progressed mainly due to Emirates' need for a replacement for its Airbus A330-243s. On 30 May 2013, Singapore Airlines became the launch customer by stating it would order 30 787-10s (provided Boeing launched the programme), to be delivered in 2018–19. Four years later, Emirates committed to procuring 40 Boeing 787-10s in two- and three-class cabins for 240–330 passengers during Dubai Air Show 2017. The agreement served the rights of Emirates to convert a part of its order to a shorter Boeing 787-9. They were planned to be adapted for 7–8.5 hour-long flights, in a 280-seat, three-class layout. Deliveries were planned from 2022.

As the engines available for both B787-9/10s could not meet Emirates' requirements, the order was about to be cancelled in early 2019. The initial 70,000–72,000lbf (310–320kN) thrust engines of the Dreamliners had insufficient power for hot Dubai and the option for more powerful 76,000lbf (340kN) turbofans was deemed uneconomic.

As Boeing Commercial Company decided to adapt new engines to meet the future need of Emirates, the airline reviewed its order and changed it to 30 Boeing 787-9s in 2019. Despite the decisions to retain the order, the Boeing 777X procurement was prioritised over the future need to replace the Boeing 777-300ERs and Airbus A380s from the mid-2020s. Four years after the last modification of the Boeing 787 order, it was modified again, this time during Dubai Air Show 2023. The new order was now for 20 Boeing 787-8s and 15 Boeing 787-10s with no timeline determined for their productions and deliveries.

The Boeing 787-8, with a typical capacity of 220 passengers, has a range of 7,355nmi (13,621km/8,464 miles). It is the base model for the Dreamliner family and first entered service in 2011. As of January 2023, approximately 26 per cent of Dreamliner orders were for the 787-8, with 386 delivered. The Boeing 787-8 has a length of 56.72m (186ft 1in) and can carry a maximum of 359 passengers in an all-economy

As of December 2023, Emirates had prioritised its orders for Boeing 777Xs over Boeing 787s. Today, Etihad Airways, another airline from the United Arab Emirates operates Boeing 787 Dreamliners including this model -10 with r/c A6-BMF. (Babak Taghvaee)

class cabin, while this is 406 and 440 for the Boeing 787-9 and 787-10 respectively. This significant increase of passenger capacity is due to the increased length of the larger model at 68.28m (224ft).

The current maximum take-off weight of the B787-8 and B787-10 are 227,900kg (502,500lb) and 250,000kg (560,000lb) thanks to the General Electric GEnx-1B or Rolls-Royce Trent 1000 turbofan engines. On the B787-8, each produces a maximum 64,000lbf (284kN) thrust and on the B787-10, each produces a maximum 76,000lbf (340kN) thrust. The current maximum range of the B787-8 is 7,355nmi (13,620km/8,460mi), and for the B787-10 it is 6,430nmi (11,910km/7,400 miles). On Emirates' B787-81Hs and B787-101Hs, these specifications will be different, as more powerful and economic General Electric GEnx-1B turbofan engines will be installed.

Airbus A380-800 Fleet: 2008–Today

To challenge the Boeing 747's dominance in the market of long-haul, wide-body passenger aircraft, in 1988, Airbus began work to develop a full-length double-deck jetliner. Two years later, the project was announced, and finally in 1994, the project designated as A3XX was presented. Later named the A380, the programme for its development was launched in full on 19 December 2000 with a total cost of €9.5 billion (US$10.7 billion). Five years later, the first prototype was unveiled at Toulouse. It flew on 27 April 2005.

Singapore Airlines, the launch customer, received the first example on 15 October 2007 and it entered service ten days later. In 2008, deliveries of the aircraft manufactured for Emirates began, and in just a few years, the airline became the largest operator of the type. Out of 254 examples produced, including three prototypes, 123 were delivered to Emirates between 2008 and 2021. As of December 2023, 90 were airworthy and 28 were stored. The recent pandemic impacted operations of the wide-body passenger aircraft and resulted in the early retirement of some.

As mentioned above, Airbus began working on the A380, an ultra-high-capacity airliner (UHCA) to compete with the Boeing 747. It was planned to be superior to the Boeing 747 in every aspect including its range and passenger capacity. The mega project, announced at the 1990 Farnborough Air Show, had a stated goal of 15 per cent lower operating costs than the 747-400, the most advanced variant of Boeing 747 at that time. Airbus organised four teams of designers, one from each of its partners (Aérospatiale, British Aerospace, Deutsche Aerospace AG and CASA) to propose new technologies for its future aircraft designs.

In January 1993, Boeing and several companies in the Airbus consortium started a joint feasibility study for a Very Large Commercial Transport (VLCT), aiming to form a partnership to share the limited market. This didn't bear fruit and the companies parted ways.

In June 1994, Airbus announced its plans for the development of the aircraft designated A3XX. At the same time, Boeing launched a project to design and develop a new, large aircraft as the successor to the Boeing 747-400; this ultimately became the Boeing 747-8. This would be was the last in the series of Boeing 747-family aircraft designed and built to compete with the Airbus A3XX (A380). The Boeing 747-8 was not as successful as the A380, with just 155 examples built, including the Boeing 747-F (freighter) examples, while Airbus produced 254 A380s (including three test aircraft).

In 2000, the projected development cost was €9.5 billion. In 2004, Airbus estimated that an additional €1.5 billion (US$2 billion) was required. To start the programme in 2000, the governments of France, Germany and the United Kingdom loaned Airbus €3.5 billion and refundable advances reached €5.9 billion (US$7.3 billion). At that time, 50 examples of the aircraft (now A380) had been ordered by six launch customers. The aircraft configuration was finalised in early 2001, and manufacturing of the first A380 wing-box component started on 23 January 2002. Major structural sections of the A380 are built in France, Germany, Spain and the UK. Due to the large size of the aircraft's parts, Airbus used its A300-600ST Beluga transport aircraft to fly them to the Jean-Luc Lagardère Plant assembly hall in

Toulouse, France. For the smaller parts, a fleet of roll-on/roll-off (RORO) ships and barges and heavy trucks were used. After assembly and completion of several test flights, the aircraft were flown to the Airbus Hamburg-Finkenwerder operations centre to be furnished and painted.

The first A380 prototype with r/c F-WWOW was completed in January 2005 and flown on 27 April. Equipped with Rolls-Royce Trent 970 turbofan engines, each producing 334.29kN (75,152lbf) take-off thrust, the aircraft flew from Toulouse–Blagnac Airport with a crew of six, headed by chief test pilot Jacques Rosay. On 25 August 2006, the first A380 prototype (an A380-861 with c/n 009) equipped with Engine Alliance GP7270 turbofan engines was test flown. Engine Alliance was a joint venture between General Electric and Pratt & Whitney and manufactured the GP7270 for the A380. With 363kN (81,500lbf) maximum thrust, this engine was more powerful than the Rolls-Royce Trent 970 of the A380-841.

In 2000, Emirates was the first airline to sign up for the Airbus A380, ordering seven with options for five more. Despite this, it received its first aircraft after Singapore Airlines received its order, due to Emirates' requirement for more powerful GP7270 turbofans. Emirates received its first A380-861 in July 2008 and used it for service between Dubai and New York in August.

In 2013, Concourse A, the world's first purpose-built A380 terminal, opened at Dubai International Airport, expanding that airport's capacity to 75 million passengers per year. Home to the Emirates' A380 fleet, Concourse A featured dedicated Emirates first- and business-class lounges with direct boarding to the upper deck of the aircraft.

Deliveries of Emirates A380-861s

The first four A380-861s were delivered in 2008 (c/n 11, 13, 16 and 20, which received r/c A6-EDA to A6-EDD). In 2009, Emirates received three more, and in 2010 it took delivery of another eight A380-861s. They received r/c A6-EDE to A6-EDO. Their c/n were 17, 7, 23, 25, 28, 9, 30, 46, 42, 56 and 57. In 2011, 2012 and 2013, Emirates received another five, 11 and 13 respectively. A6-EDP, A6-EDQ, A6-EDR, A6-EDS and A6-EDT with c/n 77, 80, 83, 86 and 90 were delivered on 14 October, 28 October, 25 November, 16 December and 2 December 2011 respectively. The aircraft delivered in 2012 had r/c A6-EDU to A6-EDZ and A6-EEA to A6-EEE. Their c/ns were 98, 101, 103, 105, 106, 107, 108, 109, 110, 111 and 112. Those delivered in 2013 had r/c A6-EEF to A6-EEQ as well as A6-EER and A6-EES. Their c/n were 113, 116, 119, 123, 127, 132, 133, 134, 135, 136, 138, 139 and 140.

Many of the innovations developed on the Emirates A380 cabin were a first for Airbus, such as showers, innovative lighting and the recent premium economy cabin. The collaboration of airline and manufacturer have shaped the identity of the A380 over the years and continues to transform the passenger experience. In late 2008, Emirates introduced 'shower spas' in first class on its A380s, allowing each passengers travelling five minutes of hot water. This required the aircraft to carry 2.5 tonnes of water (usually 60 per cent was used).

The first five A380s (A6-EDA to A6-EDE) had 14 first class, 76 business class and 399 economy seats, while the next seven, with r/c A6-EDF to A6-EDL, had a larger number in economy class at 427 passengers.

In 2014, Emirates received 13 A380-861s: A6-EEQ (c/n 141) on 14 February, A6-EET (c/n 142) on 27 March, A6-EEU (c/n 147) on 27 March, A6-EEV (c/n 150) on 19 May, A6-EEW (c/n 153) on 27 June, A6-EEX (c/n 154) on 9 July, A6-EEY (c/n 157) on 4 September, A6-EEZ (c/n 158) on 22 August, A6-EOA (c/n 159) on 26 September, A6-EOB (c/n 164) on 4 November, A6-EOC (c/n 165) on 26 November, A6-EOD (c/n 168) on 10 December, and A6-EOE (c/n 169) on 22 December 2014.

In 2015, Emirates received 15 A380-861s with r/c A6-EOF to A6-EOT. Their c/n were 171, 172, 174, 178, 182, 184, 186, 187, 188, 190, 200, 201, 202, 203 and 204.

In 2016, Emirates received 20 more A380s. They were A6-EOU (c/n 205) on 26 January, A6-EOV (c/n 206) on 19 February, A6-EOW (c/n 207) on 25 March, A6-EOX (c/n 208) on 13 April, A6-EOY (c/n 209) on 22 April, A6-EOZ (c/n 2010) on 20 May, A6-EUA (c/n 211) on 30 May, A6-EUB (c/n 213) on 21 June, A6-EUC (c/n 214) on 10 September, A6-EUD (c/n 216) on 30 June, A6-EUE (c/n 217) on 19 August, A6-EUF (c/n 218) on 5 October, A6-EUG (c/n 219) on 25 October, A6-EUH (c/n 220) on 18 November, A6-EUJ (c/n 222) on 30 November, A6-EUK (c/n 223) on 9 December, A6-EUL (c/n 224) on 20 December, A6-EUM (c/n 225) 28 December, A6-EUN (c/n 226) on 29 December and A6-EUO (c/n 227) on 29 December.

A6-EDS is an A380-86 with GP7270 turbofan engines. It is at Charles de Gaulle Airport on 22 September 2023. (Babak Taghvaee)

This aircraft first flew with temporary r/c F-WWAG on 28 October 2011 and exchanged it for r/c A6-EDV upon delivery on 30 July 2012. It is at Charles de Gaulle Airport after arriving from Dubai on 7 October 2023. (Babak Taghvaee)

This A380-861 with r/c A6-EDW was delivered on 30 August 2012. It is departing Dubai International Airport for Paris on 14 February 2015. (Babak Taghvaee)

Another image of A6-EDW at Dubai International Airport, this time on 25 November 2014. (Babak Taghvaee)

Airbus A380-861 with r/c A6-EEC was delivered on 30 November 2012. The aircraft is owned by Doric Asset Finance and has been operated under a long-term leasing contract. The aircraft was stored at Dubai World Central (DWC) between 20 July 2020 and 17 October 2022 during the pandemic. It is at Paris on 2 September 2023. (Babak Taghvaee)

This A380-861 was delivered to Emirates on 28 December 2012. It is landing at Charles de Gaulle Airport on 22 September 2023. (Babak Taghvaee)

This A380-861 with r/c A6-EEI first flew with temporary r/c F-WWAM on 17 February 2013. It was delivered on 17 June 2013 and received a special 'Unit for Wildlife' livery in November 2015, although this was later removed during maintenance. It is at Paris on 22 September 2013. (Babak Taghvaee)

First flown on 24 June 2013 and delivered on 12 December, A6-EEP is an Emirates A380-861. It is in Istanbul in September 2023. (Riza Aksoy)

A6-EEQ has been operated since 14 February 2014. It also carried the 'United for Wildlife' special livery. It is taking off from Dubai on 15 February 2015. (Babak Taghvaee)

A6-EEU is one of two A380-861s painted blue with 'Dubai Expo' special markings. This one received its special livery in September 2021. It is often flown to European capitals and is seen at Paris on 23 November 2023. (Babak Taghvaee)

A6-EEW was the second Airbus A380-861 with 'Expo 2020 (Sustainability / Green)' livery applied in April 2018. It is at Charles de Gaulle Airport on 22 August 2023. (Babak Taghvaee)

Delivered on 9 July 2014, A6-EEX is another A380-861 at Paris in December 2023. (Babak Taghvaee)

This Airbus A380-861 with r/c A6-EOA, operated by Emirates since 26 September 2014, had a 'Real Madrid' special livery applied in December 2015 but as you can see in this image, taken in Paris in 2023, it has been removed. (Babak Taghvaee)

Airbus A380-861 with r/c A6-EOB, delivered on 4 November 2014, taking off from Dubai International Airport in February 2015. (Babak Taghvaee)

A6-EOP was damaged severely when it fell off jacks at Emirates Maintenance Center in Dubai in August 2019. It was repaired and returned to service in March 2020 but quickly put into store during the pandemic. It returned to the sky on 11 March 2023. It is at Charles de Gaulle Airport on 18 April 2016. (Babak Taghvaee)

A6-EOT has been in service with Emirates since 24 December 2015. The aircraft carried a special livery for the 'Paris Saint-Germain' football team in 2016. It is taking off from Larnaca after an emergency landing (on medical grounds) on 19 April 2016. (Babak Taghvaee)

These images show 'Paris Saint-Germain' livery on the port and starboard sides of A380-861 with r/c A6-EOT in April 2016. (Babak Taghvaee)

Airbus A380-861 with r/c A6-EOU once had 'Expo 2020 (Opportunity / Orange)' special colours, which were applied in July 2018. It is taking off from Paris in December 2020. (Babak Taghvaee)

A380-861 with r/c A6-EOU with regular livery in Paris on 19 November 2023. (Babak Taghvaee)

A6-EOW, an A380-861, at Paris in October 2023. (Babak Taghvaee)

This image shows A380-861 with r/c A6-EUB landing at Paris with thrust reversers of its number 2 and 3 GP7270 turbofan engines activated. It has been in use by Emirates since 21 June 2016. (Babak Taghvaee)

A6-EUF, an A380-861, is taking off from Paris in November 2023. (Babak Taghvaee)

This A380-861 with r/c A6-EUG was delivered to Emirates on 25 October 2016 and is taking off from Munich in 2023. (Babak Taghvaee)

In August 2022, this A380-861 with r/c A6-EUJ received a 'Journey to the Future' special livery, illustrating a seven-storey pillarless landmark in Dubai's Museum of the Future. The aircraft is at Paris in September 2023. (Babak Taghvaee)

A6-EUK is another Airbus A380-861 carrying the 'Journey to the Future' livery on its fuselage. (Babak Taghvaee)

Trent 972-Equipped A380-842s

In 2010, Airbus announced that it was working on improving the A380 model to increase its maximum take-off weight as well as its range. The new A380-800 series, which Airbus had intended to complete from 2013, incorporated a strengthened airframe structure and a 1.5 degree increase in wing twist. The series was to have an improved maximum take-off weight, thus providing a better payload/range performance. The A380s had an increased maximum take-off weight by 4 tonnes (8,800lb), to 573 tonnes (1,263,000lb) and the range was extended by 100nmi (190km/120 miles) thanks to a reduced flight load, which was achieved with optimised fly-by-wire control laws.

In 2013, British Airways and Emirates became the first customers to receive A380s with these improvements. In addition, Emirates requested that Airbus study the feasibility of upgrading the engines to be competitive with the Boeing 777X around 2020. However, since the decision had been made to terminate the A380's production, no further development took place.

Beginning with the A380 with c/n 225 delivered to Emirates in December 2016, Rolls-Royce Trent 972-84/972B-84 turbofan engines were fitted. This change altered the aircraft's name designation to A380-842. The last 33 A380s for Emirates were equipped with these engines, each producing a maximum 356.81kN (80,213lbf) thrust.

Back in 2015, Emirates had signed a contract for 200 Trent 900s, including long-term service support, at a cost of US$9.2 billion or US$46 million per engine. Some of these engines were installed on the aircraft with r/c A6-EUM–A6-EUZ and A6-EVA–A6-EVS.

In 2017 nine A380s were delivered, including A6-EUI (c/n 221) on 21 February, A6-EUP (c/n 228) on 25 March, A6-EUQ (c/n 229) on 12 May, A6-EUS (c/n 234) on 30 November, A6-EUT (c/n 236) on 1 November, A6-EUV (c/n 239) on 6 November, A6-EUX (c/n 241) on 28 July, A6-EUY (c/n 242) on 29 August and A6-EUZ (c/n 244) on 29 September. Eight more were delivered in 2018, including A6-EUR (c/n 232) on 16 March, A6-EUU (c/n 238) on 30 June, A6-EUW (c/n 240) on 14 September, A6-EVA (c/n 167) on 26 April, A6-EVB (c/n 162) on 16 November, A6-EVE (c/n 250) on 28 November, A6-EVF (c/n 252) on 7 December and A6-EVH (c/n 257) on 14 December.

In January 2018, Emirates confirmed the order for 36 A380s, but the deal was thrown back into question in October over a disagreement regarding engine fuel burn. As this order could have ensured production of the A380 beyond 2028, its cancellation led to the closure of the A380 production line after completion of the 123rd and final A380-861 for Emirates. In February 2019, when Airbus announced that it was going to end production of the A380, Emirates had replaced its order for A380s with 40 A330-900s and 30 A350-900s (the A330s were later cancelled). At the time of the announcement, Airbus had 17 A380s on its order book to complete: 14 for Emirates and three for All Nippon Airways.

On 25 September 2020, Airbus completed the final A380 fuselage (c/n 272), which was delivered with r/c A6-EVS on 16 December 2021. At that time, eight A380s ordered by Emirates (including c/n 272) and one A380 ordered by All Nippon Airways were still waiting to be delivered in 2020 and 2021.

In 2019, 2020 and 2021, Emirates received its last six, three and five A380-842s respectively. They increased the total number of the aircraft type in its service to 123. Those delivered in 2019 were A6-EVC (c/n 248) on 7 May, A6-EVD (c/n 249) on 19 July, A6-EVG (c/n 256) on 18 June, A6-EVI (c/n 258) on 12 December, A6-EVJ (c/n 259) on 8 November and A6-EVK (c/n 260) on 20 December; those delivered in 2020 were A6-EVL (c/n 261) on 4 December, A6-EVM (c/n 264) on 11 December and A6-EVN (c/n 267) on 22 December; while those delivered in 2021 were A6-EVO (c/n 268) on 18 June, A6-EVP (c/n 269) on 12 May, A6-EVQ (c/n 270) on 7 October, A6-EVR (c/n 271) on 10 December and A6-EVS (c/n 272) on 16 December.

In December 2023, 58 of its 123 aircraft of the type were still being operated under long-term leasing contracts. They were A6-EDF, A6-EDG, A6-EDH, A6-EDP to A6-EDT, A6-EDV to A6-EDZ, A6-EEB, A6-EEC, A6-EEI to A6-EEP, A6-EER to A6-EET, A6-EEY, A6-EOA, A6-EOB, A6-EOE, A6-EOF, A6-EOL to A6-EON, A6-EOP to A6-EOS, A6-EOU, A6-EOV, A6-EOX to A6-EOZ, A6-EUA to A6-EUD, A6-EUF, A6-EUI, A6-EUL, A6-EUN to A6-EUR, A6-EUU, A6-EUV and A6-EUX to A6-EUZ.

This is the first A380 built by Airbus, an -841 model with Trent 970 turbofan engines. This aircraft with r/c F-WWOW was used to test Trent 972 turbofan engines before Airbus constructed the first A380-842 prototype originally equipped with the engine. (Babak Taghvaee)

A6-EVC is an Airbus A380-842 with Trent 972 turbofan engines. It is landing at Heathrow Airport in December 2023. (Babak Taghvaee)

Delivered on 18 June 2021, A6-EVO is an A380-842. It is a frequent flyer to London but was photographed in Paris in 2020. (Babak Taghvaee)

During the opening ceremony of every Dubai Air Show, two Emirates aircraft fly together with the Al-Fursan aerobatic display team of the UAE Air Force over DWC or Al-Maktoum Airport. A Boeing 777-31HER with r/c A6-EPP is in front, and A380-842 with r/c A6-EUZ behind. Both had 'Year of Zayed 2018' special liveries for the opening ceremony in November 2017. (Ramin Bamaboulo)

A380-842 with r/c A6-EUZ is flying in formation with the Aermacchi MB-339NAT advanced jet trainers of the Al-Fursan display team during the opening ceremony of Dubai Air Show 2017. (Ramin Bamboulo)

Retirement of the A380s

In 2020, Emirates grounded the majority of its aircraft due to the restrictions imposed on air travel as a result of the pandemic. Most A380s were put into storage. In 2019, Emirates' A380s logged a total 61,679 flights out of 121,210 flights of the airline that year. In 2020, five were retired. The airline logged 13,113 flights with an average number of 13 airworthy A380s in 2021.

As countries began relaxing restrictions on air travel, Emirates reactivated many of its A380s and averaged 924 weekly flights with its aircraft in 2022, increasing to 935 in 2023. However, this was still less than the average 1,127 weekly flights in 2019.

As of September 2019, Emirates initiated its A380 retirement plan by withdrawing two aircraft that were due for a major overhaul and using them for spares. There was no demand in the second-hand market. Since the retired aircraft had already been fully written down, there was no residual value. As further aircraft were retired, Emirates-owned airframes continued to be used for parts, while leased airframes were returned to their lessors. One such return to lessor Doric was purchased by Emirates for £25.3 million in late 2022, for spare parts. Amedeo, an A380 lessor, started to find a use for them after their lease expiration.

The five A380s retired in 2020 were all -861 models with GP7270 turbofan engines that had accumulated significant flying hours, and their overhaul was not economic. They were A6-EDA, A6-EDB, A6-EDD, A6-EDF and A6-EDH starting in February 2020 with the rest following in March.

Future of the A380 Fleet

Out of 118 A380s currently in service with Emirates, 27 were not active in December 2023. Some were stored at Al-Maktoum International Airport, Dubai, while others were under depot maintenance or overhaul (C and D checks) leaving 91 examples airworthy. The inactive aircraft were A6-EDC, A6-EDE, A6-EDG, A6-EDI, A6-EDJ, A6-EDL, A6-EDN, A6-EDP, A6-EDR, A6-EDT, A6-EDX, A6-EEH, A6-EEQ, A6-EQQ, A6-EOY, A6-EUK, A6-EUN, A6-EUP, A6-EUZ and A6-EVA. Among these, A6-EOO and A6-EOU were under heavy maintenance at Toulouse, while ten others were under maintenance at Dubai. The remaining 15 aircraft were stored, awaiting decisions to be made about their future. R/c A6-EDC to A6-EDJ were to be used for parts and scrapped in 2024 and 2025.

Under a US$2 billion programme, 67 A380s will have their cabins retrofitted by the end of 2024. On 6 January 2023, A6-EVM, with its retrofitted cabin, was deployed on the Dubai to Heathrow service, operating as EK003. On this occasion Sir Tim Clark, President of Emirates, said:

> Customers will notice the difference the moment they step onboard – the spacious A380 will look and feel even more impressive and comfortable. With our latest interiors and products, this newly refurbished aircraft elevates our inflight experience in all classes of travel and enables us to offer more premium economy seats to meet customer demand. I'm particularly proud that this refurbishment work was designed, conducted and completed in house at our facilities in Dubai, to the highest standards of quality and safety. It reflects the world class aviation capabilities and infrastructure that exists within Emirates, and here in the UAE.

The retrofitted cabin features 56 premium economy class seats on the main deck, and new colour palettes evident in the carpeting and wall panels. On the upper deck, first and business class seats sport cream leather upholstery and lighter-toned wood finishing. The brand's signature ghaf tree motif also features prominently throughout the interiors, including hand-stencilled panels in the first-class shower spa.

This A380-861 with r/c A6-EDH was retired from service in March 2020. It was stored at Al-Maktoum Airport until it was scrapped in 2023. It was the 6,000th Airbus aircraft built and because of that, a special sticker was added to its livery in January 2010 when it was delivered to Emirates. (Babak Taghvaee)

As the programme progressed, engineers worked simultaneously on two aircraft. This meant that one aircraft in the fleet was being withdrawn from service every eight days and transferred to Emirates Engineering facilities in Dubai. A6-EUW was the second aircraft to have its cabin retrofitted in January 2023. Each retrofitted cabin had seating for 484 passengers (14 first class, 76 business class, 56 premium economy and 338 economy seats). As of December 2023, 25 A380s had been retrofitted including A6-EUE, A6-EUH, A6-EUJ, A6-EUL, A6-EUS, A6-EUU, A6-EUV, A6-EUW and A6-EVC to A6-EVS. This cabin retrofit will allow the aircraft to remain in service until 2035. In total, 53 Boeing 777-300ERs were retrofitted in 2023.

This A380-861 with r/c A6-EDR has been in service with Emirates since 25 November 2011. The aircraft belongs to Doric Asset Finance and has been stored at Al-Maktoum Airport for years and is now earmarked for retirement and as a source of spare parts. (Babak Taghvaee)

A6-EDL is one of more than 20 A380-842/861s currently stored in Dubai and awaiting scrapping or stripping for parts. This aircraft has been in storage there since 21 July 2020. (Babak Taghvaee)

The first-class seats of the Airbus A380. (Emirates)

Economy seats in an Airbus A380. (Emirates)

Airbus A350-900 Fleet: 2024–Future

By the end of 2024, Emirates will operate the Airbus A350-941 long-range, wide-body twin-engine jet airliner, an aircraft acquired to be operated alongside the Boeing 787-8/10. It is intended to operate as a replacement for some of the four-engined Airbus A380-861 wide-body airliners earmarked for retirement in 2024 and 2025. When this book was written, Emirates had a firm order for 15 A350-941s with an option for 15 more.

The A350 was designed and developed by Airbus in 2004 as a response to the Boeing 787 Dreamliner. It was a development of a successful A330 wide-body airliner but with composite wings and new engines. The project for design and development of the aircraft began under the name of 'XWB' which stood for (eXtra Wide Body). The aircraft was planned to be powered by two Rolls-Royce Trent XWB high bypass turbofan engines.

On 6 October 2005, the programme's industrial launch was announced with an estimated cost of almost €3.5 billion. Based on the A330's design, it was planned initially to be a 250–300-seat wide-body aircraft using mostly aluminium-lithium alloys instead of carbon-fibre-reinforced polymer (CFRP) in the fuselage. On 14 July 2006, during the Farnborough International Air Show, Airbus announced that it had redesigned the programme, under which it had now named the A350 XWB, drawing the attention of various airlines including Singapore Airlines, which agreed to order 20 with options for another 20.

Under the A350 XWB design, the aircraft had a wider fuselage cross-section, allowing various seating configurations for a maximum capacity of 440–475 passengers. The redesigned fuselage also had composite material used in many of its parts, allowing a higher cabin pressure and humidity and lower maintenance costs. On 1 December 2006, the Airbus board of directors approved the industrial launch of the A350-800, -900 and -1000 variants.

The two-year delays caused by design changes increased the total cost of the programme from US$5.3 billion (€5.5 billion) to approximately US$10 billion (€9.7 billion), increasing the price of each aircraft to almost double its original price and forcing Airbus to re-negotiate with buyers who had already placed orders. Airbus later announced that the aircraft's fuselage would have composite frames on its structure with aluminium strips for electrical continuity as a safety measure for protection against lightning strikes.

Qatar Airways, Emirates' rival in the Middle East, purchased A350 wide-body passenger aircraft in 2005. Emirates sought an improved design and decided against ordering the initial version of the A350. Several years later, the company ordered 50 Airbus A350-900s and 20 stretched versions known as A350-1000s. It selected Trent XWB turbofan engines for them.

In 2011, after Airbus redesigned the A350-1000 with higher weights and a more powerful engine variant to provide more range for trans-Pacific operations, Emirates cancelled its order for 70 A350s and instead increased its A380 orders. In early November 2017, Emirates committed to purchase 40 Boeing 787-1000 aircraft before Airbus presented an updated A350-900 layout, with the rear pressure bulkhead pushed back by 1m (2.5ft).

Later, with the change in design of the A350-941 and the increase of its passenger capacity, Emirates finally purchased the aircraft. During the Dubai Air Show in November 2019, Emirates finalised an order for 50 A350-941s for US$16 billion at list prices, to be delivered from 2023 to 2028. In 2020, this order was reduced to 30 with an option for 40 A330neos (A330-900s), which were compensating for a cancelled order for 39 more A380s. According to Airbus Commercial's database, Emirates had a firm order for 15 A350-941s and an option for 15 more in December 2023. In December 2023, five A350-941s were under production at Airbus Industrie's facility in Toulouse. They had c/n 684, 693, 694, 695 and 696. The first had already received r/c A6-EXA with both of its Trent XWB-84 turbofan engines installed. It is scheduled for delivery in 2024.

The A350-941 is the first model of the A350 family. It weighs 280 tonnes (620,000lb) and has a maximum range of 8,100nmi (15,000km/9,300 miles). It is capable of carrying a maximum 440 passengers but usually is configured with two-class cabin seatings for 315 passengers (48 business and 276 economy). Emirates will also configure the aircraft with tri-class cabin seatings for 290 to 300 passengers. With a pair of Trent XWB-84s, each with 84,200lbf (375kN) net take-off rating, and 71,400lbf (318kN) net maximum continuous thrust, the aircraft will have a Mach 0.85 (488kN/903km/h/561mph) typical cruise speed and a Mach 0.89 (513kN/950km/h/591mph) maximum cruise speed.

F-WWCF is the second A350-941, with c/n 002. It was tested by Emirates in 2017. It first flew on 26 February 2014 and has been painted in 'Carbon' livery. It is landing at Al-Maktoum Airport, Dubai, in November 2017. (Babak Taghvaee)

The fourth A350-941 prototype (c/n 004) with r/c F-WZNW first flew on 26 February 2014 but was put in storage at Tarbes on 12 February 2016. It is still there, with both of its Trent XWB-84 turbofan engines removed. (Babak Taghvaee)

Chapter 3

Emirates Sky Cargo

Boeing 747-400F Fleet: 2001–17

Emirates SkyCargo is a separate entity from its parent company, Emirates. Established in October 1985, it was the world's fourth largest cargo airline worldwide in terms of the total freight tonne-kilometres flown. What made this possible was its small fleet of 13 Boeing 777F (freighter) aircraft and also the massive fleet of Emirates' Airbus A380-842/861s and Boeing 777-31HER/36NERs, which could be utilised to carry large cargo.

Established in October 1985, SkyCargo handled more than 10,000 tonnes of freight during the first year of its operations. It leased the entire freighter fleet from Emirates while also taking over management of the cargo holds in all of Emirates' passenger aircraft. In 1989, Emirates SkyCargo received an international award for its success in cargo airlift operations. It then won almost 100 other awards, and for 20 years remained the best cargo airline of the Middle East. On 3 October 1993, Emirates SkyCargo signed an agreement with EC International to handle all cargo shipments from the United States to 24 countries and regions serviced by Emirates – the Middle East, the Indian sub-continent, Europe and the Far East.

As Emirates expanded its passenger aircraft fleet and increased the number of its flights and routes, Emirates SkyCargo also increased and expanded its activities in 1997. In that year, SkyCargo experienced growth accounting for 16 per cent of the Emirates Group revenue.

Emirates Sky Cargo only used Emirates passenger aircraft to carry air freight until 2001, after which the airline began leasing cargo aircraft. In 2005, the airline also started operating its own cargo aircraft. Emirates began leasing a Boeing 747-47UF heavy transport aircraft from Atlas Air on 9 February 2001. Painted in the colours of Emirates SkyCargo, the aircraft with c/n 29261 kept its American r/c N408MC during its wet-lease by Emirates. It was operated by the crew of Atlas Air.

The Boeing 747-47UF that Emirates leased was a Boeing 747-400F (freighter), an all-freight version of the Boeing 747-400 wide-body and long-haul passenger aircraft. While using the updated systems and wing design of the passenger versions, it featured the original short upper deck of the classic Boeing 747s to reduce weight. With a maximum take-off weight of 397,000kg (875,000lb) it can carry a maximum 124,000kg (274,100lb) of cargo. The model's first aircraft flew on 4 May 1993 and entered service with Cargolux on 17 November 1993.

Atlas Air was and still is one of the major operators of this aircraft type. It received 14 Boeing 747-47UFs including ten equipped with side cargo doors (SCD) in addition to the nose cargo doors between 1999 and 2002. In addition, the airline owned or leased many other Boeing 747-400Fs including former passenger Boeing 747-400s that had been converted to cargo aircraft.

The Boeing 747-400Fs, including those in use with Atlas Air, had a main deck nose cargo door and a mechanised cargo-handling system. The nose door, which swings up, allows loading and unloading containers up to 12m (40ft) on motor-driven rollers at the base of the cargo floor. Those Boeing 747-400Fs with SCD could carry dimensionally taller cargo modules. In addition, a lower deck or belly side door also allows loading of unit load devices (ULD) up to 1.63m (5.34ft) tall.

Emirates SkyCargo has operated six different Boeing 747-400Fs. Four were leased from Atlas Air and the other two from ASL Airlines Belgium. N415MC (c/n 32837) was the second Boeing 747-47UF that Emirates SkyCargo operated from August 2003. This example had a side cargo door in addition to the one in the nose. During the years of operation, Emirates SkyCargo often chartered Boeing 747-200F cargo aircraft that could carry a maximum 110 tonnes of cargo, about ten tonnes less than that carried by the Boeing 747-400F series aircraft. In August and December 2004, Emirates SkyCargo began leasing N497MC and N498MC, an Atlas Air Boeing 747-47UF and a Boeing 747-47UF SCD.

A year later, Emirates SkyCargo began operating Airbus A310-308F cargo aircraft. Three were procured and received between July 2005 and January 2006, allowing Emirates to expand its fleet of cargo aircraft to seven. In the financial year ending March 2006, SkyCargo announced revenues of more than $1 billion and carried more than one million tonnes of cargo. In the same year, the airline also launched a freighter service to Barcelona, using the Airbus A310-308Fs.

Satisfied with the operations of the Boeing 747-400Fs, Emirates SkyCargo signed for ten Boeing 747-8F aircraft, to be powered by General Electric's GEnx jet engines, in a deal worth US$3.3 billion. The aircraft were to be obtained through a leasing contract with Dubai Aerospace Enterprise (DAE). DAE was the owner, while Emirates SkyCargo would lease the aircraft for at least ten years. Emirates then reduced its order for Boeing 747-8Fs to five and converted the balance to an order for Boeing 777-200Fs, which the airline had operated since 2009. Then in December 2012, Emirates also cancelled its order for five Boeing 747-8Fs to focus on operating only Boeing 777-200Fs.

With the deliveries of more Boeing 777-200Fs, Emirates returned its Boeing 747-47UFs to their lessor Atlas Air. In addition to these, N498MC was the first to have its wet-leasing contract terminated in February 2008 followed by N497MC, N415MC and N408MC in June 2012, February 2013 and April 2013 respectively.

However, Emirates SkyCargo continued to use the type. In May 2016, it wet-leased two Boeing 747-4HAFs from ASL Airlines Belgium. The aircraft with r/c OO-THC (c/n 35235) and OO-THD (c/n 35236) were both equipped with General Electric CF6-80C2B5F turbofan engines (four per aircraft). Each had been built in 2007. Both were returned to their lessor in June and December 2017. All of the Boeing 747-400Fs leased by Emirates SkyCargo were still airworthy as of December 2023.

This Boeing 747-47UF with r/c N408MC was the first aircraft of its kind to be leased by Emirates SkyCargo. The aircraft was operated by SkyCargo between February 2001 and April 2013. This image shows it at Frankfurt in April 2007. (Martin Ortle)

Emirates SkyCargo operated this Boeing 747-47UF SCD of Atlas Air with r/c N498MC between January 2005 and February 2008. It is at Frankfurt Airport, Germany, in 2007. (Martin Ortle)

This Boeing 747-47UF with r/c N415MC was another side cargo door variant that Emirates SkyCargo leased from Atlas Air. SkyCargo used the aircraft from August 2003 until September 2012. It is in Amsterdam on 20 March 2008. (Paul Daly)

This aircraft with r/c OO-THC was one of two Boeing 747-4HAFs of ASL Airlines, Belgium (originally from Aircastle Ltd), which Emirates SkyCargo operated. The aircraft was leased from Aircastle Ltd and was operated by ASL Airlines for Emirates SkyCargo between May 2016 and August 2017. (Howard Chaloner)

OO-THD was the second Boeing 747-4HAF that Emirates SkyCargo leased. The 2008-built cargo aircraft was leased by Emirates SkyCargo twice between 2008 and 2017. It is at Heathrow Airport on 27 February 2016. (Vin LK – LKs Away Days)

Airbus A310-300F Fleet: 2005–09

An Airbus A310-308F with r/c A6-EFA was the first owned Emirates SkyCargo aircraft, which entered service in June 2005. It was one of three A310-308s previously leased to Aeroflot by Airbus between 1992 and 2004. Due to their low cycles and flying hours, they were earmarked for conversion into freighters. While A6-EFA (c/n 646) was converted to cargo aircraft at Dresden between October 2004 and June 2005, the other two with c/n 592 and 622 were converted to freighters later. Emirates purchased them all as passenger aircraft and sent them to Dresden to be converted. The other two received r/c A6-EFB and A6-EFC in service with Emirates. Conversion of A6-EFB took place between November 2005 and April 2006, while A6-EFC was converted a few months later.

The Airbus A310-300F was a short- to medium-range wide-body twin-engine jet airliner developed and manufactured by Airbus. The freighter had the capacity to carry 39,000kg (78,000lb) of freight over a distance up to 5,950km (3,697 miles). The aircraft had a maximum payload of 40,600kg (89,507lb). The main cargo deck can hold up to 16 standard pallets each 2.24 x 3.17m. The underfloor hold can carry either 14 LD3 containers or three 2.24 x 3.17m pallets and six LD3 standard containers.

In the early 1990s, Airbus had converted A310-200 wide-body passenger aircraft to A310-200F freighters. The first was delivered in 1994; however, due to its lesser fuel capacity and weaker engines, it had a shorter range and lower payload than the A310-300. This led to the creation of the A310-300F by converting former A310-300 passenger aircraft to cargo aircraft, with FedEx one of the first and major users. For Emirates SkyCargo, the A310-300F was a cost-effective and economic aircraft to operate due to the commonality of its maintenance and spare-parts support with Emirates' A310-300s and A300B4-600Rs.

A6-EFB was one of three Airbus A310-308Fs operated by Emirates SkyCargo between 2005 and 2008. (Aero Icarus)

A6-EFC was the third Emirates SkyCargo A310-308F operated between 2006 and 2009. It is at Zurich on 9 July 2006. (Aero Icarus)

When the three cargo A310s entered service, Emirates still had one A310-300 passenger aircraft in its service (A6-EKL). The aircraft flew to Asian destinations, particularly Pakistan, until May 2007, when it was retired and sold back to Airbus Financial Services.

SkyCargo also retired its three A310-308Fs from service in 2008 and 2009. A6-EFA was retired in October 2008, followed by A6-EFB and A6-EFC in December 2008 and March 2009 respectively. These aircraft were equipped with General Electric CF6-80C2A8 turbofan engines, one of the most powerful and fuel-efficient variants of their kind installed on A310s. Buyers were found quickly; Kuzu Airlines Cargo, a Turkish cargo airline, purchased all three and registered them as TC-LER, TC-SGM and TC-VEL respectively. A few years later, the company was rebranded as ULS Airlines Cargo. As of December 2023, all three A310-308Fs were airworthy.

The converted A310 freighter provided a quickly available and cost-effective cargo transport for mid-size freight. Its low empty weight and wide body with large fuselage cross-section enables fast and efficient cargo handling and good freight volume. Despite that, Emirates SkyCargo replaced them with Boeing 777F (-200F), which were more cost-effective and economic to maintain due to their commonality with the large fleet of Emirates Boeing 777-21HER/21HLR wide-body passenger aircraft.

Boeing 777F (-200F) Fleet: 2009–Today

Emirates SkyCargo has operated Boeing 777F wide-body long-haul cargo aircraft, which are based on the Boeing 777-200LR (long range) wide-body passenger aircraft. The aircraft is capable of carrying a maximum 103,700kg (228,619lb) and can fly to a maximum range of 9,750nmi (18,057km/11,220 miles) or 4,970nmi (9,200km/5,720 miles) at its maximum structural payload.

Boeing designed and developed the 777-200F or 777F (freighter) as a replacement for the cargo 747-200Fs, McDonnell Douglas DC-10s and McDonnell Douglas MD-11Fs. In 2005, Air France showed interest in acquiring it as a replacement for its remaining fleet of classic 747-200F series.

The 777F features a new supernumerary area, which includes four business-class seats forward of the rigid cargo barrier, full main deck access, bunks and a galley. As the aircraft promises improved operating economics compared to older freighters, airlines have viewed the 777F as a replacement for freighters such as the Boeing 747-200F, McDonnell Douglas DC-10 and McDonnell Douglas MD-11F. For Emirates SkyCargo, the Boeing 777F was used as a replacement for Airbus A310-308Fs and the Boeing 747-400F series wide-body cargo aircraft.

On 20 November 2005, Emirates announced orders for eight Boeing 777 freighters, with the first scheduled for delivery in 2007. Emirates received its first, classified Boeing 777F1H (1H is Boeing's customer code for Emirates) with r/c A6-EFD, on 27 March 2009. The aircraft, with c/n 35606, was owned by DAE Capital, which also procured nine more Boeing 777Fs for dry-leasing to Emirates SkyCargo.

All Boeing 777Fs were delivered with a pair of General Electric GE90-110B1L turbofan engines. As of April 2021, 247 freighters had been ordered by 25 different customers, with 45 unfilled orders. Operators had 202 777Fs in service as of 2018.

Between 2009 and 2022, Emirates SkyCargo received 14 more Boeing 777Fs, with r/c A6-EFE, A6-EFG–A6-EFO, A6-EFS and A6-EFT. Emirates SkyCargo received them between 12 June 2009 and 1 July 2022.

SkyCargo retired the aircraft that had accumulated the most flying hours and cycles. So far, four of Emirates SkyCargo's 15 Boeing 777F1Hs have been retired (A6-EFD–A6-EFG). Their last return flights took place on 25 January 2019, 29 April 2019, 25 June 2021 and 24 August 2022 respectively.

Two of the four were sold, while two remain the property of DAE Capital. A6-EFD was sold to Titan Aviation Holdings Inc, which leased it to Southern Air and then Atlas Air with r/c N704GT. A6-EFE, which remained owned by DAE Capital, was leased to Kalitta Air with r/c N772CK from 12 June 2019. A6-EFF was leased to Lufthansa Cargo with r/c D-ALFJ from September 2021, and A6-EFG was sold to AeroLogic and has a new r/c, D-AALU, from 24 August 2022.

Back in 2006, Emirates SkyCargo chose the Boeing 747-8F as its future heavy cargo aircraft and subsequently ordered ten via DAE Capital, although five were cancelled and converted to orders for Boeing 777Fs. In December 2012, the order for the initial five Boeing 747-8Fs was cancelled and also converted to Boeing 777F. Eight of the current 11 Boeing 777Fs of Emirates SkyCargo are those procured by DAE Capital. An all-Boeing 777F fleet reduced the maintenance and operational costs for Emirates SkyCargo and increased its profitability.

Following the restrictions imposed on air travel during the pandemic in 2020, Emirates SkyCargo utilised Emirates passenger aircraft for cargo. On 24 June 2020, the airline started using 14 Boeing 777-31HER/36NERs as cargo aircraft by removing seats from the economy class cabin. In November of that year, SkyCargo started flying A380-842/861s as temporary freighters known as 'mini freighters' to provide additional capacity. These joined the Boeing 777-31HER/36NERs that had already been converted to cargo aircraft. Each A380 could carry 50 per cent of the cargo carried by the Boeing 777Fs.

To relieve some of the passenger aircraft from cargo duty, Emirates placed an order for two additional Boeing 777Fs during the Dubai Air Show in November 2021. A6-EFT and A6-EFU were delivered in May and June 2022 respectively. Then, on 8 November 2022, Emirates SkyCargo announced another firm order for five more Boeing 777Fs with two to be delivered in 2024 and three in 2025. Once delivered, some of the current Boeing 777F1Hs of Emirates SkyCargo will be retired and returned to their lessors.

This Boeing 777F with r/c A6-EFN has been in use by Emirates under a long-term leasing contract since June 2014. It is at Charles de Gaulle Airport in September 2023. (Babak Taghvaee)

A6-EFO is a Boeing 777F and is at Frankfurt in December 2023. (Babak Taghvaee)

First flown on 10 March 2013, A6-EFK is a Boeing 777F1H in use by Emirates SkyCargo under a leasing contract with DAE. It is at Heathrow Airport on 13 October 2018. (Vin Lk)

A6-EFI, a Boeing 777F1H has been operated by Emirates since 29 November 2012. The aircraft is the property of DAE. (Mike Kell)

Another image of Emirates SkyCargo's Boeing 777F1H with r/c A6-EFO (c/n 42233) this time at Hamburg in June 2019. (Mike Kell)

A6-EFH, an Emirates Boeing 777F1H, has been operated by the airline since 28 September 2012 and is at Heathrow Airport in May 2019. (Mike Kell)

This Boeing 777-F1H was operated by Emirates SkyCargo between 2009 and 2019. After its return to its lessor, DAE Capital, it was leased to Kalitta Air. It is at Zurich in January 2012. (Martin Ortle)

Emirates SkyCargo leased this Boeing 777F1H from DAE Capital between 2012 and 2022. The aircraft has been in use by AeroLogic since 24 August 2022. It is at Frankfurt Airport (Rhein-Main AB) in August 2016. (Martin Ortle)

A6-EFD was one of the first Boeing 777F1Hs operated by Emirates SkyCargo. It was leased from DAE Capital between 27 March 2009 and 25 January 2019. It is in Los Angeles on 6 August 2015. (Ron Monroe)

Another image of Boeing 777F1H with r/c A6-EFO, this time at Los Angeles on 16 August 2015. (Ron Monroe)

Emirates SkyCargo has been using this Boeing 777F1H with r/c A6-EFS under a long-term leasing contract since 3 September 2015. It is at Los Angeles on 4 May 2017. (Ron Monroe)

Appendix 1

Incidents and Accidents

Emirates has earned a reputation for offering industry-leading services on the latest and most efficient wide-body aircraft in the skies, and this success is underpinned by safety, which is always the airline's priority. The group has dedicated teams, policies, programmes and safety management systems to assess and mitigate risks, embed safety practices across its businesses, and engage employees to influence the organisational safety culture. As a result, the group's airline, SkyCargo airline and Flight Training Academy have had a healthy rate of safety reporting through its activities.

Only three major accidents and incidents have taken place in the airline's history:

- On 20 March 2009, an A340-541 with r/c A6-ERG (c/n 608) had an accident during take-off from Melbourne Airport. The accident happened due to improper planning by the aircraft's pilot and co-pilot during a reduced-rate take-off. The aircraft had a tail strike on the runway and collided with the airport's lighting and the instrument landing system (ILS). The pilots declared an emergency and returned to the airport safely. The aircraft was repaired and returned to service.
- On 3 August 2016, a Boeing 777-31H with r/c A6-EMW (c/n 32700) flew from Thiruvananthapuram International Airport, India, to Dubai, UAE, with flight EK521. The accident took place during an attempted go-around at Dubai Airport. All 300 on board survived. One firefighter was killed while trying to put out a fire in the aircraft after landing. The cause of the accident was determined to be the pilot's mistake as both engine thrust levers, and therefore the engine thrust, remained at idle during the attempted go-around, except for the last three seconds prior to impact.
- On 22 August 2019, A6-EOP (c/n 200), an A380-861 sustained serious damage to its nose section in a maintenance mishap at the airline's maintenance centre in Dubai. The aircraft's nose landing gear apparently retracted, causing the nose to hit the ground. The aircraft was repaired and returned to service.

Appendix 2

Emirates Group Fleet Details

Fleet in December 2023

Aircraft type	Operator	Owned	Leased	On order*
Cirrus SR22 G6	Emirates Flight Training Academy	22	-	-
Diamond DA-42-VI	Emirates Flight Training Academy	3	-	-
Embraer Phenom 100EV	Emirates Flight Training Academy	5	-	-
A319-115X CJ	Emirates Executive	1	-	-
Airbus A350-941	Emirates	-	-	65
Airbus A380-842	Emirates	26	7	-
Airbus A380-861	Emirates	37**	50***	-
Boeing 777-F1H	Emirates SkyCargo	2	9	5
Boeing 777-21HLR	Emirates	8	2	-
Boeing 777-31HER	Emirates	91	24	-
Boeing 777-36NER	Emirates	-	8	-
Boeing 777-81H	Emirates	-	-	35
Boeing 777-91H	Emirates	-	-	170
Boeing 787-81H	Emirates	-	-	20
Boeing 787-101H	Emirates	-	-	15
Total	4	195	100	310

* Including both firm orders and options for future orders.

** Three owned A380-861s are being cannibalised for their parts in DWC airport.

*** Two leased A380-861s are being cannibalised for their parts in DWC airport.

Historic Fleet (Including Subsidiary Airlines)

Aircraft type	Total number used	First introduction	Last removed from fleet
Airbus A300B4-203	1	1985	1988
Airbus A310-304	4	1987	2000
Airbus A310-308	6	1992	2007
Airbus A310-308F	3	2005	2009
Airbus A330-243	29	1999	2016
Airbus A340-313	8	2004	2016
Airbus A340-541	10	2003	2016
Airbus A380-861	3	2008	2020
Boeing 727-2K5	1	1989	1993
Boeing 727-2M7	1	1985	1996
Boeing 727-264	1	1988	1995
Boeing 737-340	1	1985	1987
Boeing 747-47UF	4	2001	2013
Boeing 747-4HAF	2	2016	2017
Boeing 777-21H	3	1996	2015
Boeing 777-21HER	6	1996	2016
Boeing 777-F1H	4	2009	2022
Boeing 777-31H	12	1999	2018
Boeing 777-31HER	23	2005	2022
Boeing 777-36NER	8	2005	2021